Prayer Thoughts

Praying Scriptures With God Power

ORVA LYNN KAUFMANN

Table of Contents

This book is dedicated
To Prayer Warriors who prayed this book into existence
the original pray-ers
Mary, Doris, and Trudy
who supported these writings
From the beginning
And to the many other pray-ers who came along side to
support the writing of the Prayer Thoughts over the years

Using Scriptures as Prayer

May my prayer be set before You as incense may the lifting up of my hands be like evening sacrifice (Psalm 141:2) How precious to me are Your thoughts, O GOD, I praise You because I am fearfully and wonderfully made, Your works are wonderful. (Psalm 139:17) For You have said "I'm precious in Your sight and because You love me, You have redeemed me, and have called me by name." You have said, "I'm yours." (Isaiah 43:1, 4) I remember the days of long ago, I meditate on all Your works and consider what Your hands have done. I spread out my hands to You. My soul thirsts for You like a parched land. (Psalm 143:5, 6) My eyes are fixed on You, O Sovereign Lord, in You I take refuge. Do not leave my soul destitute. (Psalm 141:8) Let the morning bring me word of Your unfailing love for I have put my trust in You. Show me the way I should go, for to You, I lift up my soul. (Psalm 143:8) Teach me Your way, O LORD, I will walk in Your truth: unite my heart to fear Your name. (fear meaning honor, reverential trust) (Psalm 86:1) Teach me Your way, O LORD,I will walk in Your truth: Teach me to do Your will; for You are my God: Your spirit is good; lead me into the land of uprightness. May Your Holy Spirit lead me? (Psalm 143:10) Because you love Me says the LORD, I will rescue you, I will protect you for you acknowledge My name. You will call upon Me, and I will answer you. I will be with you in trouble; I will deliver you and honor you.

(Psalm 91:14-15) "For You have hemmed me in behind and before, You have laid Your hand upon me. Such knowledge is too wonderful." Psalm 139:5

"Praise the LORD. Praise the LORD, O my soul. I will praise the LORD all my life; I will sing praise to my God as long as I live. Do not put your trust in princes, in mortal men, who cannot save. Blessed is he whose hope is in the LORD his God, the Maker of heaven and earth, the sea, and everything in them – the LORD, *who remains faithful forever*." Psalm 146:1-3, 5b-6

All verses from the NIV

My Thoughts

Helpful Steps to use for Prayer

"God uses the prayers of Christians to bring about
His work on earth"
E.M. Bounds

Prayer is communicating and communing with God our
Heavenly Father. Sometimes we need a little help getting
started. Based on the LORD's Prayer here are four steps that
can be helpful in getting you started in your daily prayer life.

Praise "Praise the LORD. Praise the name of the LORD,
Praise Him" Psalm 135:1 "I will praise you, O LORD among the
nations; I will sing of You among the peoples, for great is Your
love, reaching to the heavens; Your faithfulness reaches to the
skies. Be exalted, O God, above the heavens; let Your glory be
over all the earth." Psalm 57:9-11 "Everyday I will praise You
and extol Your name forever and ever." Psalm 145:2

Repent "If we confess our sins, He is faithful and just to
forgive us our sins, and to cleanse us from all unrighteousness."
I John 1:9 for "there is not one who does not sin." II Chronicles
6:36b "If I cherish sin in my heart the LORD would (will) not
listened." Psalm 66:18,Matthew 4:17

Ask "The eyes of the LORD are on the righteous and His ears are attentive to their cry." Psalm 34:15 "Ask, and it shall be given you; seek and you shall find; knock, and it shall be opened unto you." Matthew 7:7-8 "The Holy Spirit helps us in our weakness. We do not know what we ought to pray for, but the Holy Spirit himself intercedes for us with groans that words cannot express. And He who searches our hearts know the mind of the Spirit, because the Spirit intercedes for the saints in accordance with God's will. Romans 8:26-27

Yield Let us pray as Jesus prayed in Gethsemane, "not as I will, but as You will." Matthew 26:39 "Submit yourselves, then to God." James 4:7 "For God, His way is perfect." Psalm 18:30a "The LORD is faithful to all His promises and loving toward all He has made. Psalm 145:136

My Thoughts

Does God Hear Me?

Prayer How many times have you prayed and wondered if God has heard your prayers. Do you cry as the Psalmist does, "O God, do not keep silent; be not quiet, O God, be not still." Psalm 83:1 But when God's answer comes back, He says for you to continue waiting. "Wait for the LORD; be strong and take heart and wait for the LORD." Psalm 27:14 "Wait for the LORD and keep His way." Psalm 37:34 "As for God, His way is perfect; the word of the LORD is flawless. He is a shield for all who take refuge in Him." 2 Samuel 22:31

Waiting is hard for us because we like instant results. God knows our impatience so He tells us, "I, even I, am He who comforts you." Isaiah 51:12 "Be still before the LORD and wait patiently for Him; do not fret." Psalm 37:7 "**Cast all your anxiety on Him** because He cares for you." 1 Peter 5:7 So, "on my bed I remember (meditate) You (my LORD); I think of You through the watches of the night. Because You are my help, I sing in the shadow of Your wings. My soul clings to You; Your right hand upholds me." Psalm 63:6-8 The LORD is good to them that wait for Him, to the soul that seeketh Him. It is good that a man should both hope and quietly wait." Lamentations 3:25-26 (KJV)

Therefore, "Devote yourselves to prayer being watchful and thankful." Colossians 4:2 "Be joyful in hope, patient in affliction, faithful in prayer." Romans 12:12 As we are waiting for the answer, **God has promised**, "I will keep in perfect peace him whose mind is steadfast, because he trusts in Me." Isaiah 26:3

"May the **God of hope** fill you with all joy and peace as you trust in Him, so that you may overflow with hope by the power of the Holy Spirit." Romans 16:27 To the only wise God be glory forever through Jesus Christ! Romans 16:27, Isaiah 26:3

My Thoughts

Lifting Up My Hands

"May my prayer be set before you like incense; May the lifting of my hands be like evening sacrifice." Psalm 121:2 "How precious to me are Your thoughts, O God, I praise you because I am fearfully and wonderfully made, your works are wonderful." Psalm 139:17

"For you have said, I'm precious in Your sight and because You love me, You have redeemed me, and have called me by name." Isaiah 43:1,4 "How precious to me are Your thoughts, O God, I praise you." Psalm 139:17a 'I remember the days of long ago, I meditate on all Your works and consider what Your hands have done. I spread out my hands to You. My soul thirsts for You like a parched land." Psalm 143:5,6 "My eyes are fixed on You, O Sovereign LORD, in You I take refuge. Do not leave my soul destitute." Psalm 143:8

"Let the morning bring me word of Your unfailing love for I have put my trust in you. Show me the way I should go, for to You I lift up my soul." Psalm 143:8 "Teach me the way, O LORD, I will walk in Your truth; unite my heart to fear (honor) Your name." Psalm 86:11 "Let the morning bring me word of Your unfailing love for I have put my trust in you. Show me the way I should go, for to You I lift up my soul." Psalm 143:8

"Teach me the way, O LORD, I will walk in Your truth; unite my heart to fear (honor) Your name." Psalm 86:11 "Teach me to do Your will for You are my God. May Your Holy Spirit lead me." Psalm 143:10 "Because You love me, **says the LORD**, I will rescue you, I will protect you for you acknowledge My name. You will call upon Me, and I will answer you. I will be with you in trouble; I will deliver you and honor you." Psalm 91:14-15 "For You have hemmed me in behind and before, You have laid Your hand upon me. Such knowledge is too wonderful." Psalm 139:5

"Praise You the LORD. Praise the LORD, O my soul." Psalm 146:1

My Thoughts

Scripture Thoughts for Our Country

My Thoughts
Scriptures to pray over our country

LIGHT THE NATION
WITH PRAYER

You are the LIGHT of the world. A city on a hill cannot be hidden. Neither do people light a lamp and put it under a bowl. Instead they put it on its stand, and it gives light to everyone. Matthew 5:15 (NIV)

Let us then approach the throne of grace with confidence, so that we may receive mercy and find grace to help us in our time of need. Hebrews 4:16 As we follow God's command to pray for our nation and our leaders: "first of all, that requests, prayers, intercession and thanksgiving be made for every one, for kings and all those in authority, that we may live peaceful and quiet lives in all godliness and holiness." I Timothy 2:1

Some ways to pray for people in authority:

that they will be God fearing and recognize that they are accountable to Him for each decision and act. Proverbs 9:10

that they will be granted wisdom, knowledge and understanding. James 1:5

that they will recognize their own inadequacy and pray and seek the will of God. Proverbs 3:5-8, Luke 11:9-13

that they will have courage to resist manipulation, pressure and the fear of man. Proverb 29:25

God our Father wants us also to pray for world leaders. Daniel prayed for Nebuchadnezzar who wanted to know the interpretation to his dream. Daniel and his friends prayed for the answer. The answer was revealed in a dream. "Then Daniel blessed the God in heaven. Daniel said, Blessed be the name of God for ever and ever: for wisdom and might are His: and He changeth the times and the seasons. He removeth kings, and setteth up kings: He giveth wisdom unto the wise, and knowledge to them that know understanding. He revealeth the deep and secret things: He knoweth what is in the darkness, and the light dwelleth with Him." Daniel 2:19-22 KJV "The King's heart is in the hand of the LORD; He directs it like a watercourse wherever He pleases. All a man's ways seem right to him, but the LORD weighs the heart." Proverbs 21:1-2 "The effective, fervent prayer of a righteous man/woman avails much" James 5:16b Elijah prayed earnestly and God answered his prayers. James 5:17-18

My Thoughts

An Intimate Talk with the LORD

P rayer is communicating and communing with God our Heavenly Father. To commune means to talk in an intimate way, which in prayer means to come to God, to listen for His voice as we meditate during our daily quiet time. "I will meditate on the glorious splendor of Your majesty, and on Your wondrous works." Psalm 145:5 "My soul yearns for You in the night; in the morning my spirit longs for You. Isaiah 26:9 "Be still before the LORD and wait patiently for Him." Psalm 37:7a "Be still and know that I AM God." Psalm 46:4 "Come my children, listen to me; I will teach you." Psalm 34:14 "My sheep listen to My voice: I know them and they follow Me." John 10:27 "Teach me to do Your will for You are my God." Psalm 143:10 "I will instruct you and teach you in the way you should go. I will counsel you and watch over you." Psalm 32:8 "I have put My words in your mouth and covered you with the shadow of My hand." Isaiah 51:16 "Whether you turn to the right or to the left, your ears will hear a voice behind you, saying, 'This is the way; walk in it.'" Isaiah 30:21

My Thoughts

What a Friend!

H ave you thought of using a hymn to communicate and commune with God our Heavenly Father? *What a Friend We Have in Jesus* is a wonderful hymn that could be used as a prayer when having your quiet time with the LORD. What a friend we have in Jesus who bears our sins and griefs. "The blood of Jesus His son cleanses us from all sin." I John 1;7 NASB "He heals the brokenhearted and binds up their wounds. Psalm 147:3 "Do not grieve, for the joy of the LORD is Your strength." Nehemiah 8:10b How wonderful that we can take everything to God in prayer! "For you are all sons (children) of God through faith in Christ Jesus." Galatians 3:26 Sometimes we forget the peace and strength we can have by prayer. "Cast your cares on the LORD, and He will sustain you." Psalm 55:22a

When we have trials and temptations, God says, "no temptation has overtaken you except such as is common to man: but God is faithful, who will not allow you to be tempted beyond what you are able; but with the temptation will also make the way of escape, that you may be able to bear it." I Corinthians 10:13 NKJV Jesus is a faithful friend who is willing to share our sorrows. "May Your unfailing love be my comfort, according to Your promise." Psalm 119:76 "The righteous cry out, and the LORD hears them; He delivers them from all their troubles." Psalm 34:17 For He knows all our weaknesses, "I will lift up my eyes to the hills from whence comes my help? My help comes from the LORD, who made heaven and earth." Psalm 121:1-2

Are we burdened with problems and cares that seem too heavy to carry? "Come to Me, all you who labor and are heavy laden, and I will give you rest." Matthew 11:28 "But they that wait upon the LORD shall renew their strength; they shall mount with wings as eagles; they shall run, and not be weary and they shall run, and not be weary; and they shall walk, and not faint." Isaiah 40:31 Jesus our precious Savior, we come to You in prayer!

"The LORD is faithful, and He will strengthen and protect you from the evil one" II Thessalonians 3:3 For in Your arms You'll take and shield us. "You hem me in behind and before; You laid Your hand upon me." Psalm 139:5 "He will cover you with His feathers and under His wings will you find refuge; His faithfulness will be your shield and rampart." Psalm 91:4

My Thoughts

First Thursday in May

The first Thursday of May has been set aside for thousands of Christians, believers in Jesus Christ, to lift their hands and voices to the LORD our God in supplication for our nation and the government that governs us; be it city, county, state or national praying for all. How wonderful it will be to participate in this event or others similar to this with so many other believers saying: "Let us then approach the throne of grace with confidence, so that we may receive mercy and find grace to help us in our time of need." Hebrews 4:16 "Praise the LORD, all you nations; extol Him, all you peoples. For great is His love toward us, and **the faithfulness of the LORD endures forever**, Praise the LORD." Psalm 117:1-2 "We will praise you O LORD among the nations; we will sing of Your love, reaching to the heavens; Your faithfulness reaches to the skies. Be exalted our LORD God, above the heavens; **let Your Glory be over all the earth**." Psalm 57:9-11

PRAY for our country, America, to return to the LORD our God, for the sins of the people of our country will be the down fall." Hosea 14:1

PRAY that the people will repent. "Even now, declares the LORD, return to Me with all your heart with fasting and weeping and mourning. Rend your heart and not your garments. Return to the LORD your God, for He is gracious and compassionate, slow to anger and abounding in love, and He relents from sending calamity." Joel 2:12-13

PRAY that we "submit ourselves (our country), then to God." James 4:7 That "God will protect us from trouble and surround us with doings of deliverance." Psalm 32:7 That "God will again have compassion on our country and will tread our sins underfoot and hurl all our iniquities into the depths of the sea." Micah 7:19 "What other nation is so great as have their gods near them the way the LORD our God is near us whenever we pray to Him." Deuteronomy 4:7

"Devote yourselves to prayer, being watchful and thankful. That God may open a door for our message so that we may proclaim the mystery of Christ." Colossians 4:2-3

My Thoughts

Our Faithful Hope

"My soul is downcast within me. Yet this I call to mind and therefore I have **hope**; because the LORD's great love we are not consumed, for His compassions never fail. They are new every morning; great is Your faithfulness. I say to myself; the LORD is my portion; therefore I will wait for Him, the LORD is good to those whose **hope** is in Him, to the one who seeks Him: It is good to wait quietly for the salvation of the LORD." Lamentations 3:20-26

"The eyes of the LORD run to and fro throughout the whole earth, to show Himself strong on behalf of those whose heart is loyal to Him." 2 Chronicles 16:9a "But we see Jesus, who was made a little lower than the angels, now crowned with glory and honor because He suffered death so that by the grace of God He might taste death for everyone." Hebrews 2:9

"Therefore since we have a great high priest who has gone through the heavens, Jesus, the Son of God, let us hold firmly to the faith we profess." Hebrews 4:14 "We have this **hope** as an anchor for the soul, firm and secure." Hebrews 6:19 "Be joyful in **hope**, patient in tribulation and faithful in prayer." Romans 12:12 "Let us hold unswervingly to the **hope** we profess, for He who promised is faithful." Hebrews 10:23

"Let us then approach the throne of grace with confidence, so that we may receive mercy and find grace to help us in our time of need." Hebrews 4:16 "I wait for the LORD, my soul waits, and in His word I put my **hope**, my soul waits for the LORD. My country put your **hope** in the LORD, for with the LORD is unfailing love and with Him is full redemption. God Himself will redeem our country from all their sins." Psalm 130:5-8

"Let our country hope in the LORD from henceforth and for-ever." Psalm 131:3

My Thoughts

Our Never Changing God

"Jesus Christ is the same yesterday and today and forever." Hebrews 13:8 "My salvation will last forever, My righteousness will never fail." Isaiah 51:6c "God has said, 'Never will I leave you; never will I forsake you.' So we say with confidence, 'The LORD is my Helper; I will not be afraid.'" Hebrews 13:5b-6

What a wonderful marvelous promises our Heavenly Father has given us through the ages that we can still claim them now in the millennium. As we are at the beginning of the millennium, let us make the commitment to communicate and commune (talk) with the LORD daily. During this daily time we can learn from the scriptures how God directs our lives, and through prayer He gives peace and joy as our faith grows in Him.

"Faith is the substance of things hoped for and the evidence of things not seen." Hebrews 11:1 "I am the LORD, the God of all mankind. Is anything too hard for Me?" Jeremiah 32:27 "For I know the plans I have for you, declares the LORD." Jeremiah 29:11a "Cast not away your confidence which hath great recompense of reward. For you have need of patience, that after you have done the will of God you might receive the promise." Hebrews 10:35-36

Thank God for answering your prayers. This daily time with the LORD will "renew (your) strength. (you) will soar on wings like eagles; (you) will run and not grow weary, (you) will walk and not be faint." Isaiah 40:31 "Through Jesus, therefore, let us continually to offer to God a sacrifice of praise the fruit of lips that confess His name." Hebrews 13:35

"May the God of peace, who through the blood of the eternal covenant brought back from the dead our LORD Jesus, that great Shepherd of the sheep, equip you with everything good for doing His will and may He work in us what is pleasing to Him, through Jesus Christ, to whom be glory forever and ever. Amen" Hebrews 13:20-21

My Thoughts

Integrating Prayer Time into Daily Life

Have you ever thought about "making prayer an integral, constant part of your daily life? To make the most of your time, take time to pray. Prayer habits are helpful tools to remind you of your dependence on God." *Our Daily Bread*

"Three times a day Daniel got down on his knees and prayed giving thanks to his God; and asking God for help." Daniel 6:10-11 Daniel was thrown into the lion's den for his continuous faithfulness in praying several times a day. He was protected from the lions because he trusted God to take care of him. David prayed morning, noon, and evening. "As for me, I will call upon God and the LORD shall save me. Evening and morning and at noon I will pray, and cry aloud, and He shall hear my voice." Psalm 55:16-17 King Manasseh called out to the LORD "in his distress sought the favor of the LORD his God and humbled himself before the God of his fathers and when he prayed to Him, the LORD was moved by his entreaty and listened to his plea." 2 Chronicles 33:12-13 "If I had cherished sin in my heart the LORD would not have listened; but God has surely listened and heard my voice in prayer. Praise be to God, who has not rejected my prayers." Psalm 66: 18-20 "Call to Me and I will answer you, and show you great and unsearchable (mighty) things which you do not know. Jeremiah 33:3

Jesus told His disciples a parable to show them that they should always pray and not give up. "In a certain city a judge who did not fear God nor regard man. Now there was a widow in that city; and she came to him, saying, 'get justice for me from my adversary.' And he would not for a while; but afterward he said within himself, 'Though I do not fear God nor regard man, yet because this widow troubles me I will avenge her, lest by her continual coming she weary me.' And the LORD said, hear what the unjust judge said. And shall not God avenge His own elect, which cry day and night unto Him, though He bear long with them? I (Jesus) tell you that He (LORD) will avenge them speedily. Luke 18:2-8 "Pray without ceasing, in everything giving thanks; for this is the will of God in Christ Jesus for you." I Thessalonians 5:17-18 "Therefore I will look unto the LORD; I will wait for the God of my salvation; my God will hear me." Micah 7:7

My Thoughts

We have Privileges

W hat a privilege we have to commune and communicate with a Living God, not made of man materials, but one who stands by His promises of caring for us at all times. As the world turns upside down with terrorists groups attacking in every part of the globe for, "sin lurks deep in the hearts of the wicked, forever urging them on to evil deeds." Psalm 36:1 We are reminded of this special privilege, "Do not be afraid of sudden terror, nor of trouble from the wicked when it comes; for the LORD will be your confidence, and will keep your foot from being caught." Proverbs 32:7 LB "He who dwells in the shelter of the Most High will rest in the shadow of the Almighty. He will cover you with His feathers, and under His wings you will find refuge: His faithfulness will be your shield and rampart. You will not fear the terror by night, nor the arrow that flies by day, nor the pestilence that stalks in the darkness nor the plague that destroys at midday." Psalm 91: 1, 4-6 As you stand firmly on these promises, "put on the full armor of God: the belt of truth, the breastplate of righteousness and your feet fitted with the readiness that comes from the gospel of peace, the shield of faith, the helmet of salvation and sword of the Spirit. Pray in the Spirit on all occasions with all kinds of prayers and requests." Ephesians 6:13-18

Pray for our leaders that they may: "Act justly, love mercy and walk humbly with God." Micah 6:8b Recognize that God alone gives wisdom and understanding, "the fear of the LORD is the beginning of wisdom." Psalm 111:10 "Would hate evil, love good, and have an attitude of humility always mindful of those they are serving, God opposes the proud but gives grace to the humble." Amos 5:14-15 Finally, pray that our leaders will "maintain an attitude of humility always mindful of those they are serving God opposes the proud but gives grace to the humble." I Peter 5:5

Pray this promise for our nation: NO weapon forged against you will prevail, and you will refute every tongue that accuses you. This is the heritage of the servants of the LORD." Isaiah 54:17

"I know the One in whom I trust, and I am sure that He is able to safely guard all that I have given Him until the day of His return." II Timothy 1:12 LB

My Thoughts

"It is impossible rightly to govern the world without God and Bible."

George Washington

J uly 4ᵗʰ is the day we celebrate our independence, the day commemorating our country becoming a nation in its own right. It is a day in which to remember the price paid over the years for freedom. Our founding fathers made a covenant with God that our nation would be built on Biblical principles.

No other time in our history has it been like this, a time when Christians need to pray diligently for our country and our leaders. Only under God's banner can we continue to have freedom and be victorious in the battles being fought around the world. "What other nation is so great as to have their gods near them the way the LORD our God is near us whenever we **pray** to Him." Deuteronomy 4:7

Paul writes "I counsel that petitions, prayers, intercessions and thanksgivings be made for all human beings, **including kings (presidents, governors) and all in positions of prominence;** so that we may lead quiet and peaceful lives, being godly and upright in everything." I Timothy 2:1-2 "For there is no authority except that which God has established." Romans 13:1b

Let us pray that our Leaders:

"**will** be men worthy of respect sincere, not indulging in much wine, and not pursuing dishonest gain, that they will keep hold of the deep truths of faith with a clear conscience. Those who serve will gain an excellent standing and great assurance in their faith in Christ Jesus." I Timothy 3:8-9,13

"**will** submit to God and be at peace with Him." Job 22:21

"**will** maintain justice and do what is right." Psalm 37:28

"**will** remember that many are the plans in a man's heart but it is the LORD's purpose that prevails." Proverbs 19:21

"**will** recognize their own inadequacy and pray and seek the will of God." Proverbs 3:5-8; Luke 11:9-13

"**will** heed their conscience, confess their sins, and repent." Proverbs 28:13; James 4:8

"**will** recognize that 'only our LORD God is worthy to receive glory and honor and power, for He created all things, and by His will they were created and have their being." Revelation 4:11

Only through the renewing of our knowledge of and faith in God through the Holy Scriptures can we be strengthen as a nation and a people

My Thoughts

LORD how Majestic
is Your Name

"O LORD our LORD, how majestic is Your name in all the earth! You have set your glory above the heavens." Psalm 8:1 "You will reign forever; You have established Your throne for judgement. You will judge the world in righteousness." Psalm 9:7 "LORD; who shall abide in Your tabernacle (God's place of dwelling)? Who shall dwell in Your holy hill? He whose walk is blameless and who does what is righteous, who speaks the truth from his heart." Psalm 15:1-2

As you come before the LORD in prayer, are you "acknowledging your sin to the LORD and not covering up iniquity. Saying, I will confess my transgressions to the LORD and He will forgive the guilt of my sin." Psalm 32:5 For "the blood of Jesus, His Son purifies us from all sin. If we confess our sins He is faithful and just and will forgive us our sins and purify us from all unrighteousness." I John 1:7b,9 How wondrous that God loves you so much that He is willing to "not remember the sins of your youth and your rebellious ways; that according to His love will remember you and instruct you in His ways." Psalm 25:5 "The LORD will reward you according to your righteousness, according to the cleanness of your hands in His sight." Psalm 18:24

During prayer time I will "meditate (speak softly to self) on Your unfailing love. Like Your name, O God, Your praise reaches to the ends of the earth; Your Right hand is filled with righteousness." Psalm 48:9-10 "As for God, His way is perfect, the word of the LORD is flawless, He is a shield for all who take refuge in Him. For who is God besides the LORD and who is the rock except our God? It is God who arms me with strength and makes my way perfect." Psalm 18:30-32

"I pray that out of His glorious riches He may strengthen you with power through His Spirit in your inner being. So that Christ may dwell in your hearts through faith. I pray that you, being rooted and established in love, may have power, together with all the saints, to grasp how wide and long and high and deep is the love of Christ, and to know this love that surpasses knowledge that you may be filled to the measure of all the fullness of God." Ephesians 3:16

My Thoughts

Keep Your Eyes On Jesus

**"Let us fix our eyes on Jesus, the author
and perfecter of our faith."**
Hebrews 12:2 KJV

August 2004 through the month of January 2005 we had hurricanes, a tsunami, flooding, and mudslides that were major disasters. The world may seem to be falling apart but Jesus says, I'm unchanging. Seek me and trust in me, rest in me, and I will bring peace to your soul. "Jesus Christ is the same yesterday and today and forever." Hebrews 13:8 Because He has said, never will I leave you; never will I forsake you, we can say with confidence, the LORD is my helper; I will not be afraid." Hebrews 13:5b6

"Do not lose heart or be afraid when rumors are heard in the land." Jeremiah 51:46; Matthew 24:6; Mark 13:7; Luke 21:9 "Who of you can by worrying can add a single hour to your life? Since you cannot do this very little thing, why do you worry about the rest?" Luke 12:25-26 Daniel trusted God when he was thrown into the lions' den. When he was taken out of the lions' den there was no manner of hurt on him because he believed God." Daniel 6:16-14 "One night the disciples were in their ship that was being tossed about by a storm. Jesus went to them walking on the sea. Peter wanted to walk on the water also. As long as Peter kept his eyes on Jesus, he was fine but when he took his eyes off of Him he sank." Matthew 14:22,23 "So fix your eyes not on what is seen, but on what is unseen. For what is seen is temporary, but what is unseen is eternal." 2 Corinthians 4:18

Therefore, "when I am afraid I will trust in God. Psalm 56:3 I will "trust in Him at all times, I will pour out my heart to Him for God is my refuge." Psalm 62:8 "He will cover me with His feathers and under His wings I will find refuge. His faithfulness will be my shield." Psalm 91:4

Thank you LORD that I will trust in you with all my heart and will not lean unto my own understanding. In all my ways I will acknowledge You, and You shall direct my paths. In the name of Jesus Christ. Proverbs 3:5-6

Thank you LORD that you will keep me safe in You as my refuge. I will praise You who counsels me; even at night You will instruct my heart. I will sing of Your strength in the morning. I will sing of Your love, my refuge in times of trouble. In the name of Jesus Christ. Psalm 16:1,7,8; Psalm 59:1

My Thoughts

"In His Presence

**"Let us acknowledge the LORD. As surely as the sun rises,
He will appear. He will come to us like the spring
rains that water earth. Hosa 6:3**

**I will rejoice in the presence of my God."
Deuteronomy 27:7**

P rayer is a time of coming into the **presence** of God the
Father. A time of worshiping and praising in His **presence.**
A time of feeling His **presence** around you.

Think of "prayer as the breath in your lungs and the blood from
your heart. The blood flows ceaselessly, breathing continues
ceaselessly; you are not conscious of it, but it is always going
on. Prayer is not an exercise, it is life, your life line to God the
Father. Praying without ceasing to keep the habit of ejacula-
tory prayer in your heart to God all the time." I Thessalonians
5:17 Oswald Chambers *My Utmost for His Highest*

"Let us come before His **presence** with thanksgiving and make
a joyful noise unto Him with psalms." Psalm 95:2 Just as cho-
lesterol clogs the arteries, so does sin clog the blood line
between God the Father and you. "Create in me a clean heart,
O God, and renew a steadfast spirit within me." Psalm 51:10
"A sinful mind is hostile to God." Romans 8:7 "You (God) have

set our iniquities before You, our secret sins in light of Your **presence**. Psalm 90:8 Sin is a veil that comes between you and being in God's **presence**. "Repent (change your mind and purpose); turn around and return (to God), that your sins may be erased (blotted out, wiped clean), that time of refreshing (of recovering from the effects of heat, of reviving with fresh air) may come from the **presence** of the LORD." Acts 3:19 Amp

"My heart (prayer) says, Seek His Face! Your Face LORD, I will seek." Psalm 27:8 "I will wait patiently for You." Psalm 40:1 "Be still and know that I AM God." Psalm 46:10 "How precious to me are Your thoughts, O God!" Psalm 139:17 "You will fill me with joy in Your **presence**." Psalm 16:11 "You have made known to me the paths of life; You will fill me with the joy in Your **presence**." Acts 2:28 "Teach us to number our days that we may gain a heart of wisdom letting the beauty of the LORD our God be upon us." Psalm 90:12,17 "In the shelter of Your **presence**, You (will) hide me from the intrigues of men; in Your dwelling You will keep me safe." Psalm 31:20

"O LORD my God, hear the cry and the prayer that I am praying in Your **presence**." II Chronicle 6:19 "I am pouring out my (prayer) heart like water in Your presence." Lamentations 2:19 "If you are pleased with me, teach me Your ways so I may know you and continue walking with You. God the Father replies, My **presence** will go with you and I will give you rest." Exodus 33:13,14

My Thoughts

Fears that Overwhelm Us

Prayer is a wonderful way of communicating with God our Heavenly Father. During this time we talk to Him about many concerns in our lives, especially the fears we have concerning money, health, and family, to name a few. Sometimes these fears overwhelm us so much that we can say as the Psalmist: "Fear and trembling have beset me, horror has overwhelmed (covered) me. Psalm 55:5 The troubles of my heart have multiplied; free me from my affliction and distress and take them away." Psalm 25:17 But God tells us that "His eyes range throughout the earth to strengthen those whose hearts are fully committed to Him." II Chronicles 16:9

And Jesus also said, "come to Me, all who are weary and burdened, and I will give you rest." Matthew 11:28 "Praise be to the LORD, to God our Savior who daily bears our burdens." Psalm 68:19 "For you have not received the spirit of bondage again to fear but you have received the spirit of adoption, whereby we cry Abba Father." I Peter 3:9 When we cry out to God, He says, "do not be afraid for I am with you; do not be dismayed, for I am your God. I will strengthen you and help you; I will uphold you with My Righteous Right hand. For I am the LORD, Your God, who takes hold of your right hand and says to you, DO NOT FEAR; I will help you." Isaiah 41:10,13

So with these promises, I can say: "The LORD is with me; I will not be afraid. The LORD is with me; He is my helper." Psalm 118:6 "The LORD is my light and my salvation whom shall I fear? The LORD is the stronghold of my life whom shall I be afraid." Psalm 27:1 God is our refuge and strength an ever present help in trouble. Therefore we will not fear, though the earth give away and the mountains fall into the heart of the sea." Psalm 46:1-2; Psalms 34, 91,121 are chock full of promises for protection and offer refuge from fears of what the now holds and the future holds.

"Let us fix our eyes on Jesus the author and finisher of our faith." Hebrews 12:2 "Who will keep you in perfect peace, you whose mind is steadfast because you trust in God." Isaiah 26:3 "For the mind controlled by the HOLY SPIRIT is life and peace." Romans 8:6b "**May the LORD of PEACE** Himself give you peace at all times and in every way. **The LORD be with you**." II Thessalonians 3:16

My Thoughts

Pentecost

"When the day of Pentecost came, they were all together in one place. Suddenly a sound like the blowing of a violent wind came from heaven and filled the whole house. They all were filled with the Holy Spirit. Acts 2:1-4

"From the day after the Sabbath, the day that you bring the sheaf of the wave offering, you shall keep count until seven full weeks have elapsed: you shall count 50 days until the day after the seventh week, then you shall bring an offering of new grain to the LORD. On that same day you shall hold a celebration, it shall be a sacred occasion for you." Leviticus 23:15-21 There were three festivals that the Israelis were to celebrate in Jerusalem: Feast of the Tabernacles in the fall; Passover in the spring; and Pentecost fifty days after the Passover.

P entecost is a Greek word meaning fiftieth. There are fifty days between the day after Passover until Pentecost. At the end of Passover Jesus rose from the grave which was the day after the Sabbath and fifty days later the Holy Spirit was given for all believers. While the disciples and others were waiting in Jerusalem for the promise of the Holy Spirit, "they continued with one accord in prayer and supplication (humble, earnest requests) Acts 2:8 On the fiftieth day, when everyone had come to Jerusalem for the Festival, the Holy Spirit, as tongues of fire lit on each believer's head enabling them to witness to the multitudes at the Festival. Acts 2:12-15 "Having believed in Jesus, you are marked with the seal of the Holy spirit, who is a deposit guaranteeing your inheritance until the redemption of those who are God's children, to the praise of His glory." Ephesians 1:13 The Holy Spirit is given to us to help us in our daily walk and talk with Jesus our LORD. "Build yourself up in your most holy faith and pray in the Holy Spirit." Jude 1:20

During your prayer time ask the Holy Spirit to help you understand the scriptures, ask Him how you should pray for others, ask Him to open your heart to the joys of fellowshipping with the LORD. "You have received the Holy Spirit which is of God; that you might know the things that are freely given to us from God, the Holy Spirit teaches you, comparing spiritual." I Corinthians 2:12-13 "The Holy Spirit helps you when you don't know what to pray for, the Holy Spirit Himself intercedes for you with groans that words cannot express. The Holy Spirit intercedes for the saints according to God's will. Romans 8;26-27 "Hope maketh not ashamed, because the love of God is shed abroad in our hearts by the Holy Spirit which is given to you." Romans 5:5 KJV Pray that with the Holy Spirit's help you will share this love of God for others, that you will be a witness to those you come in contact with.

"Whoever is thirsty, let him/her come, let him/her take the free gift of the water of life." Revelation 33:17

My Thoughts

Perceptions of God

Have you ever thought about what your perceptions of God are? Do you consider Him to be omniscient, omnipotent, the God of creation? Or is He a vague shadowy person? "To whom then will you liken God? Or with what likeness will you compare Him? To whom then will you liken Me, that I should be equal to him says the Holy One. Have you not known? Have you not heard. The everlasting God, the LORD, the Creator of the ends of the earth, does not faint or grow weary. There is no searching for His understanding. For God is the King of all the earth: sing your praises with understanding; God reigns over the nations; God is seated on His holy throne. For the LORD God is a sun and shield; The LORD will give grace and glory; no good thing does He withhold from those whose walk is blameless." Isaiah 40:18; Acts 17:19; Isaiah 40:28; Psalm 47:7-9; Psalm 84:11

Throughout the scriptures God has revealed Himself in many ways. "God's voice thunders in marvelous ways; He does great things beyond our understanding." Job 37:5 "The heavens declare the glory of God; the skies proclaim the work of His hands" Psalm 19:1 "There is no one holy like the LORD; there is one besides You; there is no rock like our God.' I Samuel 2:2 God had many names in the Hebrew which were translated into our English Bibles as God or LORD. Some of the Hebrew names are:

Jehovah-rophe means God who heals, to restore, cure or heal physically as well as spiritually "He healed all the sick. This was to fulfill what was spoken through the prophet Isaiah: He took up our infirmities and carried our diseases. Matthew 8:16b-17

Jehovah-jireh means the LORD who sees or God's provision for us. "Righteousness from God comes through faith in Christ Jesus to all who believe; for all have sinned and fall short of the glory of God and are justified freely by His grace through redemption that came by Christ Jesus." Romans3:22-23

Jehovah-nissi means His banner over me. "The LORD is my banner." Exodus 17:15

Jehovah-robi means God is my shepherd. "I am the good shepherd. The good shepherd lays down his life for the sheep" John 10:11

"Lift your eyes to the heavens, look at the earth beneath; the heavens will vanish like a smoke, the earth will wear out like a garment and its inhabitants die like flies. But My salvation will last forever, My Righteousness will never fail." Isaiah 51:6 "May the God of peace, who through the blood of the eternal covenant brought back from the dead our LORD Jesus, that great Shepherd of the sheep, equip you with everything good for doing His will, and may He work in you what is pleasing to Him, through Jesus Christ, to whom be glory for ever and ever. Amen Hebrews 13:20-21

My Thoughts

Joyous Celebration

This is the season for joyous celebrations and elaborate preparations. We put so much energy into getting ready for the celebration of Jesus' birthday that we forget about preparing for His coming again. Jesus told the parable of the ten virgins and preparations for the bridegroom. Five of the virgins were ready but five weren't. "Jesus said, therefore keep watch, because you do not know the day or the hour. For as lightening that comes from the east is visible in the west, so will be the coming of the Son of Man. The Son of Man coming on the clouds of the sky with power and great glory. The trumpet of God will sound with His loud command, with the voice of the archangel and the dead in Christ will rise first and those of us who are alive will be caught up together with them in the clouds to meet the LORD in the air." Matthew 25:13; I Thessalonians 4:13-18; Matthew 24:30-31; Luke 21:25-29

All through the Bible, God our Heavenly Father has left instructions so that we may prepare for this glorious second coming of His Son. During our prayer time, we are to: "meditate day and night that we may observe and do according to all that is written in the Word of the LORD." Joshua 1:8 "Through Jesus, let us continually offer to God a sacrifice of praise and so worship Him acceptably with reverence and awe." Hebrews 12:28 "sing to Him, sing praises to Him; meditate on and talk of all

His marvelous deeds and devoutly praise them." Psalm 105:2 Amp "Seek, inquire of and for the LORD and crave Him and His presence (continually in our lives)." Psalms 105:4 Amp "To be still before the LORD and wait patiently for Him." Psalm 37:7

"**Blessed** (happy, fortunate, prosperous, and enviable) is the one who walks and lives not in the counsel of the ungodly (following their advice, their plans and purposes), nor stands (submissive and inactive) in the path where sinners walk, nor sits down (to relax and rest) where the scornful (and the mockers) gather. But whose delights and desire are in the law of the LORD, and on His law (precepts, the instructions, the teachings of God), who habitually meditates (ponders and studies) by day and by night." Psalm 1:1-2 Amp

Therefore, "dear friends, build yourselves up (founded) on your most holy faith and praying in the Holy Spirit; guard and keep yourselves in the love of God; expect and patiently wait for mercy of our LORD Jesus Christ (the Messiah) (which will bring you) unto life eternal. Jude 1:20 Amp

My Thoughts

Let Us Sing unto the LORD

"O Come, let us sing unto the LORD; let us make a joyful noise to the rock of our salvation. Let us come before His Presence with thanksgiving, and make a joyful noise unto Him with psalms." Psalm 95:1-2 "Thou wilt shew me the path of life: in Your presence is fullness of joy: at Your Right hand there are pleasures for evermore." Psalm 16:11

Having a prayer time requires a discipline and concentration (focus on God). Most believers down through the ages have found setting time aside first thing in the morning helps with the disciplining and concentration of your mind, soul, and spirit to put God first. You have less distractions to make your mind wonder.

"If you are struggling in prayer, it is because the wiles of the enemy are getting the upper hand and you must look for the cause of it in the lack of discipline in yourself. 'Be vigilant; because your adversary the devil, as a roaring lion, walketh about seeking whom he may devour. Resist stedfast in the faith and through prayer.' I Peter 5:8 KJV When you suspend your own activities and get down at the foot of the Cross and meditate there, God brings His thoughts to us by the Holy Spirit and interprets them to us. 'Praying always with all prayer and supplication in the Spirit.' Ephesians 6:18 You need a reliance on the Holy Spirit for help in praying. The whole source of your strength is receiving, recognizing and relying on the Holy Spirit. "I will put my Spirit within you and cause you to walk in my statutes, and you shall keep My judgments, and do them.' Ezekiel 36:27 'For as many as are led by the Spirit of God, they are the sons of God.' Rom 8:14 'Not by might, nor by power but by My spirit says the LORD of Hosts.' Zechariah 4:6 "For He guards the course of the just and protects the way of His faithful." Proverbs 2:8 Oswald Chambers, *Prayer a Holy Occupation*

"Now therefore, if you will obey My voice indeed, and keep My covenant (prayer time, communication with Me, the LORD) then you shall be a peculiar treasure unto Me above all people: for the earth is Mine." Exodus 19:5

My Thoughts

Jesus is the Reason

"Praise be to GOD and Father of our LORD Jesus Christ, the Father of compassion and the GOD of all comfort, who comforts us in all our troubles, so that we can comfort those in any trouble, with comfort we ourselves have received from GOD." 2 Corinthian 1:3-4

*J*esus *is the reason for the season*. The time before December 25th is called Advent. The four weeks before Christmas is observed by some Christians (believers) as a season of prayer and fasting. Others let the hustle and bustle of shopping, preparation, and pageantry to interfere with this time of getting ready for the Christ Child's birth. Will you become so caught up in the exciting glittery outward façade of what the world considers Christmas to be, not taking time to meditate on what Christmas really means?

"Come and see what God has done, how awesome His works on man's behalf." Psalm 66:5 "A Savior has been born! He is Christ the LORD." Luke 2:11 "For God so loved the world that He gave His only begotten Son, that whosoever believes in Him shall not perish but have eternal life." John 3:16

"In hope of eternal life, which God that **cannot lie**, promised before the world began; but hath in due times manifested His word through preaching, which is committed unto me according to the commandment of God our Savior." Titus 1:2-3 KJV

Jesus is the Reason. "Because of the LORD's great love we are not consumed for **His compassions** never fail. They are **new every morning**; great is Your Faithfulness. The LORD is good to those whose hope is in Him, to the one who seeks Him; it is good to wait quietly for the salvation of the LORD." Lamentations 3:22,23,25,26

Jesus is the Reason. "Looking for the blessed hope, and the glorious appearing of the great God and our Savior Jesus Christ.' Titus 2:13 As you pray and meditate during this time of preparation to celebrate **Jesus is the Reason,** ask your Heavenly Father how you can share this wonderful free gift of love to others. For Jesus has come that we might have life and to have it more abundantly. (John 10:10) How can they, the unbelievers, know unless we tell them? As the light of the star lead the wise men to Jesus in Bethlehem, so let **the light of Jesus shine forth from you, showing the way to the Messiah, Jesus Christ, whose birth we are celebrating.**

My Thoughts

My Prayer to You, My God

"May my prayer be set before You like incense; May the lifting of my hands be like evening sacrifice." Psalm141:2 "How precious to me are Your thoughts, O God, I praise You because I am fearfully and wonderfully made, Your works are wonderful." Psalm 139:17 "For You have said, 'I'm precious in Your sight and because You love me, You have redeemed me, and have called me by name.' You have said, 'I'm Yours.'" Isaiah 43:1-4 "How precious to me are Your thoughts, O God, I praise You." Psalm 139:17a I remember the days of long ago, I meditate on all Your works and consider what Your hands have done. I spread out my hands to You. My soul thirsts for You like a parched land." Psalm 143:5-6 "My eyes are fixed on You, O Sovereign LORD, in You I take refuge. Do not leave my soul destitute." Psalm 143:8

"Let the morning bring me word of Your unfailing love for I have put my trust in you. Show me the way I should go, for to You I lift up my soul." Psalm 143:8 "Teach me the way, O LORD, I will walk in Your truth; unite my heart to fear (honor) Your name.' Psalm 86:11 "Teach me to do Your will for You are my God. May Your Holy Spirit lead me." Psalm 143:10 "Because You love me, says the LORD, I will rescue you, I will protect you for you acknowledge My name. You will call upon Me, and I will answer you. I will be with you in trouble; I will deliver you and honor you." Psalm 91:14-15

For you have hemmed me in behind and before, you have laid Your hand upon me. Such knowledge is too wonderful." Psalm 139:5 "Praise you the LORD, Praise the LORD, O my soul." Psalm 146:1

My Thoughts

In **Quietness and Stillness**

I s this how you approach the LORD each morning or evening? Or do you come to Him with chattering with many requests, not giving the LORD a chance to talk with you? The LORD, our Heavenly Father, finds it very hard, just as we do, to talk with someone who does all the talking and no listening.

The LORD, our Heavenly Father, asks us to come before Him in stillness. (Zachariah 2:15) Can you think of sitting still and quietly focusing on one verse? Jesus said, "come with Me by yourself to a quiet place and get some rest." Mark 6:31 "Resting in the LORD and wait patiently for Him. Lifting your soul to Him." Psalm 37:7a Can you say "my soul waits in silence for God alone?" Psalm 62:1 Can you say "my soul waiteth for the LORD; He is my help and shield" for all my daily needs. Psalm 62:5 KJV He is asking you to "be silent before Him, the Sovereign LORD." Zephaniah 1:7 To be still and know "I am God." Psalm 46:10 "For this is what the Sovereign LORD the Holy One says: In repentance and rest is your salvation, in quietness and trust is your strength." Isaiah 30:15

"Wait on the LORD: be of good courage and He shall strengthen your heart: wait I say on the LORD." Psalm 27:14 During this quiet time of waiting "the LORD searches your heart and examines your mind. .Jeremiah 17:10a "He will show you His ways and teach you His paths. He will lead you in the truth and teach you for He is your God on whom you wait." Psalm 25:4-5 "The LORD is good to those waiting for Him, to those who are seeking Him. It is good to wait patiently for the saving help of the LORD." Lamentations 3:24-25

"The fruit of righteousness will be peace; the effect of righteousness will be quietness and confidence forever." Isaiah 32:17

"For those who wait upon the LORD shall renew their strength; they shall mount up with wings as eagles; they shall run and not be weary, they shall walk, and not faint." Isaiah 40:31 "May the God of peace who through the blood of the eternal covenant brought back from the dead our LORD Jesus, that great Shepherd of the sheep, equip you with everything good for doing His will, and may He work in you what is pleasing to Him through Jesus Christ, to whom be glory for ever and ever. Amen " Hebrews 13:20

My Thoughts

Sanctified

"The very God of peace sanctify you wholly; and I pray God your whole spirit and soul and body be preserved blameless unto the coming of our LORD Jesus Christ." I Thessalonians 5:23

Sanctify means to make holy, to be free from sin. Sanctified means dedicated, consecrated, made holy. "If we are to be sanctified, it must be by the God of peace Himself. The power that makes the life of the saint does not come by our efforts at all, it comes from the heart of God of peace. Sanctification is an instantaneous, continuous work of God; immediately we are related rightly to God it is manifested instantly in spirit, soul, and body." Oswald Chambers *His Upmost for His Highest*

"What? Know you not that your body is the temple of the Holy Ghost which is in you, which you have of God, and you are not your own? For you are bought with a price; therefore glorify God in your body, and in your spirit, which are God's." I Corinthians 6:19-20 In order to come into our prayer closet as holy we need to confess our sins that separate us from God, our Heavenly Father, because God is a Holy God. Every sin is a reproach to God. "For God hath not called us unto uncleanness, but unto holiness." I Thessalonians 4:7 "Wash me thoroughly from mine iniquity and cleanse me from my sin. For I acknowledge my transgressions. Create in me a clean heart, O

God; and renew a right spirit within." Psalm 51:2-3a,10 With the cleansing of our spirit and soul, "we have full freedom and confidence to enter into the (Holy of) Holies (by the power and virtue) in the blood of Jesus. And since we have (such) a great and wonderful and noble Priest (who rules) over the house of God. Let us draw near with a true (honest and sincere) hearts in unqualified assurance and absolute conviction engendered by faith (by that leaning of the entire human personality on God in absolute trust and confidence in His power, wisdom, and goodness, having our hearts sprinkled from a guilty (evil) conscience, and our bodies cleansed with pure water." Hebrews 10:19,21-22 Amp

"He that is righteous let him be righteous still and he that is holy, (sanctification, to set apart for God) let him be holy still." Revelation 22:11 Amp "To this end He established your hearts unblameable in holiness before God, even our Father, at the coming of our LORD Jesus Christ with all His saints." I Thessalonians 3:13 KJV

My Thoughts

Do You Not Know?

D o you realize that Satan "your enemy prowls around like a roaring lion looking for someone to devour." I Peter 5:8 Do you realize that you need to "be on guard so that you may not be carried away by the error of lawless men (who are controlled by Satan)." II Peter 5:17b AMP "Do not be wise in your own eyes; fear (honor) the LORD and shun evil." Proverbs 3:7 "Flee the evil desires and pursue righteousness, faith, love and peace along with those who call on the LORD out of pure heart." II Timothy 2:22

Satan uses your imagination to create distressing scenes and to make you fearful. "Do not let your heart be troubled, let the **peace of God** rule in your heart." John 14:1 "He will keep you in perfect peace who trust in Him, whose thoughts turn often to the LORD." Isaiah 26:3 LB "He can rescue you from every evil attack." II Timothy 4:18a

Therefore, "put on the full armor of God so that you can take your stand against the devil's schemes. For your struggle is not against flesh and blood, but against the rulers, against the authorities, against the powers of this dark world and against the spiritual forces of evil in heavenly realms. Stand firm then with the belt of truth buckled around your waist, with the breastplate of righteousness in place, and with your feet fitted with the readiness that comes from the gospel of peace. In addition to all this, take up the shield of faith, with which you can extinguish all the flaming arrows of the evil one. Take the helmet of salvation and the sword of God." Ephesians 6:11-17

"The LORD will fight for you; you need only to stand still." Exodus 14:14 So "be strong and courageous. Do not be afraid or terrified. For the LORD your God goes with you; He will never leave you nor forsake you." Deuteronomy 31:6 "The peace of God which transcends all understanding, will guard your (pounding) heart and your (whirling) mind in Christ Jesus." Philippians 4:7 AMP The quietness of peaceful thoughts is the first answer God gives to you when you are needy. "The LORD delights in you who fear (honor) Him, who puts hope in His unfailing love. He grants peace to your borders." Psalm 147:11,14a

May your prayers be a fragrant offering, an acceptable sacrifice, pleasing to God. And God will meet all your needs according to His glorious riches in Christ Jesus. To God and Father be glory forever and ever. Amen." Philippians 4:18b-20

My Thoughts

To Be Filled in the Morning

"In the morning You hear my voice, O LORD; in the morning I prepare (a prayer of sacrifice) for You and watch and wait (for You to speak to my heart)." Psalm 5:3 "To the children of God by faith in Christ Jesus." Galatians 3:25

Are you preparing your heart to listen to what God has to say to you concerning events that will be happening in your life this day or any other day? "Is the desire of your soul for His name, and to the remembrance of God? With your soul, do you desire God in the night; yea, with your spirit within you do you seek Him early?" Isaiah 26:8-9 Are you preparing yourself to walk with God each and every day with the help of the Holy Spirit? God said, "I will put My spirit within you, and cause you to walk in My statutes, and you shall heed My ordinances and do them." Ezekiel 36:27 "There is a spirit in man: and the inspiration of the Almighty giveth you under-standing." Job 32:8 KJV As it is written in Isaiah 64:4 and I Corinthians 2:9, "NO eye has seen, no ear has heard, no mind has conceived what God has prepared for those who love Him, but God has revealed it to you by His Spirit." The Holy Spirit is gentle and "will guide you in truth: He shall not speak of himself; but whatsoever He shall hear, that shall He speak: and He will show you things to come." John 16:13 "The Spirit searches all things even the deep things of God, no one knows the thoughts of God except the Spirit of God. You have not received the spirit of the world but the Spirit who is from God, that you may understand what God has freely given us." I Corinthians 2:10-11

How can you love God unless you spend time getting to know Him as God of creation and the lover of your soul? "The reverent fear and worship of the LORD is the beginning of wisdom and skill (the preceding and the first essential, the prerequisite and the alphabet): a good understanding, wisdom, and meaning have all those who do (the will of the LORD). Your praise of Him endures forever." Psalm 11:10 Amp "The works of the LORD are great, sought out by all those who delight in them." Psalm 111:2

Therefore, "Your word have I hid in mine heart, that I might not sin against You. I will delight myself in Your statutes: I will not forget Your word. Turn my eyes away from worthless things. My eyes stay open through the watches of the night, that I may meditate on Your promises." Psalm 119:11,16,37,48

"For this cause we also, since the day we heard it, do not cease to pray for you, and to desire that you might be filled with the knowledge of His will in all wisdom and spiritual understanding. That you might walk worthy of the LORD unto all pleasing, being fruitful in every good work, and increasing in knowledge of God." Colossians 1:9-10

My Thoughts

AWAKE! AWAKE!

"Could you not wait and watch with Me for one hour? Watch and pray so that you will not fall into temptation. The spirit is willing but the body is weak." Mark 14:37

These words of Jesus are just as important today as they were in the Garden of Gethsemane. Jesus wants you to "prepare your mind for action, be self-controlled; set your hope fully on the grace to be given you when Jesus Christ is revealed. Live your life as a stranger here in reverent fear (loving reverence for God, a reverential trust and belief in His promises, with a hatred of evil) for you are redeemed from an empty way of life with the precious blood of Christ, a lamb without blemish or defect." I Peter 1:17 Amp Prepare yourself through prayer and studying the Word of God, "continue to live in Him, rooted and built up in Him (daily prayer and knowing the Word of the LORD), strengthen in faith as you were taught and overflowing with thankfulness." Colossians 2:6-7 Amp

Behold I (Jesus) will come as a thief. Blessed are you who watcheth, and keepeth your garments on (the Righteousness of Jesus by the covering of His blood), lest you walk naked (spiritually naked), and they see your shame." Revelations 16:15 KJV Say to God "create in me a clean heart and renew a steadfast spirit within me. Restore to me a joy of Your salvation and grant me a willing spirit to sustain me." Psalm 51:10,12 "Then Your Righteousness will go before me and the glory of the LORD will be my rear guard. Then call on Me, I (God your Father) will answer.' Isaiah 58:8b Say to God, "LORD I have heard of Your fame; I stand in awe of Your deeds, renew them in my day, in my time make them known." Habakkuk 3:2 "Those who fear the LORD talked with each other and the LORD listened and heard. A scroll of remembrance was written in His presence concerning those who feared the LORD and honored His name." Malachi 3:16

"And this is my prayer that your love may abound more and more in knowledge and depth of insight so that you may be able to discern what is best and may be pure and blameless until the day of Christ, filled with the fruit of righteousness that comes through Jesus Christ to the glory and praise of God." Philippians 1:9

My Thoughts

The LORD of Peace

"May the LORD of Peace Himself give peace at all times and in every way. The LORD is with you." II Thessalonians 3:16

Peace, peace, where can I find peace? Are your thoughts and your everyday activities causing you distress? Trials and tribulations seem to follow you, causing you anxiety and turmoil. "Be careful, or your heart will be weighed down with the anxieties of life." Luke 21:34 "You who walk in the dark, who has no light, trust in the name of the LORD and rely on your God." Isaiah 50:10 "Jesus says, Come unto Me all you who are weak and burdened and I will give you rest (inner peace)." Matthew 11:28

"Love righteousness and hate iniquity, God will anoint you with oil of gladness." Psalm 45:8 "The fruit of righteousness will be peace, the effect of righteousness will be quietness and confidence forever." Isaiah 32:11 The LORD himself will go before you and will be with you; He will never leave you nor forsake you, do not be afraid; do not be discouraged." Deuteronomy 31:8

"The LORD will fight for you, you need only to stand still." Exodus 14:14 "Blessed are you who trusts in the LORD." Psalm 84:12 "Peace I leave with you; My peace I give you. I do not give to you as the world gives. Do not let your heart be troubled and do not be afraid." John 14:27 "He will keep you in perfect peace, whose mind (thought, imagination) is steadfast because you trust in Him. Trust in the LORD forever, the LORD, is the Rock eternal." Isaiah 26:3,4 "Let the peace of God rule in your heart." Colossians 3:15

"May you listen to what God the LORD says; He promises peace to His people, His saints His salvation is near those who fear Him, that His glory may dwell in your heart. Love and faithfulness meet together; righteousness and peace kiss each other. The Eternal God is your refuge and underneath you are His everlasting arms." Psalm 85:8-10; Deuteronomy 33:27

My Thoughts

May Adonai Bless You

May Adonai (God) bless you and keep you. May Adonai (God) make His face shine on you and show you His favor. May Adonai (God) lift up His face toward you and give you peace. Numbers 6:24-26

This is the benediction (invocation of blessing) given at the end of the Sunday morning or Saturday services. It is the most recognizable of all the blessings in the New and Old Testaments. There are many blessings throughout the Bible that can be used in your prayers for individuals in your life; such as your children, spouse, co-workers, neighbors, church ministries and missions, or people who are angry with you.

According to Rolf Garborg in his book *The Family Blessing* there are **four types of blessings** found in the Scriptures:

A **blessing spoken by God** to the people. The benediction by God in Numbers 6:14-16

A **blessing spoken by people to God**. When we speak well of or express praise to God, then you are blessing Him, like David did in Psalm 103:2 "Bless the LORD, O my soul, and forget not of His benefits." Paul wrote in Ephesians 1:3 "Blessed be the God and Father of our LORD Jesus Christ, who has blessed us with every spiritual blessing." "O LORD, You are my God. I will exalt you and praise your name for in perfect faithfulness you have done marvelous things, things planned long ago." Isaiah 25:1

A **blessing spoken by God or people over things**. Deuteronomy 28 is filled with blessings by God over material resources if you obey Him. In Matthew 14:19-21, Jesus blessed the fishes and loaves, calling down God's miraculous power to multiply them.

A **blessing spoken by one person to another**. Jesus told His disciples, "Bless those who curse you, pray for those who mistreat you." Luke 6:28 "When you are cursed bless, when you are slandered, answer kindly". I Corinthians 4:12-13 Jesus, also, blessed His disciples in Luke 24:50 and blessed the little children in Mark 10:16

A **blessing for you:** that you will have clear direction from our Heavenly Father as you listen to Him daily:

In the name of Jesus Christ: I bless your going out and your coming in today and everyday. May you ponder the way of your feet and not turn to the right or to the left from the path that God has planned for you. May you have clear direction of the road you are to walk today. When you allow the LORD to direct your steps, He takes delight in each move you make. May you understand the lessons He is trying to teach you from what He permits to happen in your life. If you stay on God's pathway, your life will be filled with joy and gladness. (Psalm 32:8; 37:23; 121:8; 143:8,10; Proverbs 4:21-23,26; 8:20) Adonai is Hebrew for the LORD our God

My Thoughts

My Soul Melts

"My soul melteth for heaviness"
Psalm 119:28 KJV

Fear What if I lose my job? **What if** everything I own is destroyed? **What if** my retirement plan has been wiped out? **What if** I get a debilitating disease? **What if** is a little phrase that can go on and on and on. <u>Fear is a very small word</u> but can cause devastating results in a person's life. Someone once said that fear stands for: <u>F</u>alse <u>E</u>vidence <u>A</u>ppearing <u>R</u>eal The little word fear is mentioned 330 times in the Bible. Sometimes it is used as **"fear the LORD"** which means to have a **reverential trust in GOD** with hatred for evil. It also includes a commitment to His Word. **"Fear the LORD, you His saints, for those who fear Him lack nothing."** Psalm 34:9 **"It is better to take refuge in the LORD than to trust in man. It is better to take refuge in the LORD than to trust in princes."** Psalm 119:8-9

Every believer through the ages **has become fearful** at some point during their life, and some being fearful all their lives. Even Paul in II Corinthians experienced harassment at every turn, conflicts on the outside, fears inside. II Corinthians 7:5 David in the Psalms expressed fear so vividly for all of us when he said, **"Listen to my prayer, O GOD, do not ignore my plea; hear me and answer me, my thoughts trouble me and I am** distraught. **My heart is in anguish with in me; horrors of death assail me. Fear and trembling have beset me; horror has overwhelmed me."** Psalm 55:1-5 **"Evening, morning, and noon I cry out in my distress and He hears my voice."** Psalm 55:17

"**Fan into flame the gift of GOD, which is in you. For GOD did not give you a spirit of timidity, of cowardice, of craven and cringing and fawning fear, but a spirit of power (to overcome), of love and of self discipline."** II Timothy 1:6-7 Amp **"Cast your cares (fears, worries) on the LORD and He will sustain you."** Psalm 55:22 **"Do not be anxious (fearful) about anything, but in everything by <u>prayer and petition</u> with thanksgiving present your requests to GOD."** Philippians 4:4-6

God called Lydia Prince, as a young woman, to go to Jerusalem with no church backing and no money to depend on to do His work. *She was totally dependent on GOD* and His promises that He would supply <u>all</u> her needs for herself and the orphan children she rescued. One instance that was written about: there was no food in the house when Lydia set the table for dinner. When asked where the food was coming from, she replied the LORD would provide by the time the children were ready to sit down to eat. **And He did**! It is an amazing true story of faith, love and the **miraculous power of prayer.** Lydia believed Jesus' words **"do not worry about your life; what you will eat, or about your body, what you will wear. Do not be afraid, for your Father knows that you have need of these things and will supply them."** Luke 12

Through daily prayer and memorizing GOD's word, you will be able to overcome fear that comes against us in any given situation. Therefore, when you pray, since you have hidden God's word in your heart, the Holy Spirit will prompt you with the right verse to make the enemy flee. **God, our Heavenly Father, reminds you "My Spirit remains among you. Do not fear!"** Haggai 2:5

Ask Abba Father to: "strengthen my feeble hands, steady my knees that give way, and say to my **fearful heart, Be strong, do not fear, I, Abba, Father will be with you through it all."** Isaiah 35:3-4

My Thoughts

In Times of Trouble

P rayer is a wonderful way of communicating with God our Heavenly Father. During this time we talk to Him about many concerns in our lives, especially the fears we have concerning money, health and family, to name a few. Sometimes these fears overwhelm us so much that we say as the Psalmist, "Fear and trembling have beset me, horror has overwhelmed (covered) me." Psalm 55:5 "The troubles of my heart have multiplied; free me from my affliction and distress and take them away." Psalm 25:17

But God tells us that "His eyes range throughout the earth to strengthen those whose hearts are fully committed to Him." II Chronicle 16:9 Jesus also said, "come to me, all who are weary and burdened, and I will give you rest." Matthew 11:28 And so even in times of trial, we can say "praise be to the LORD, to God our Savior who daily bears our burdens." Psalm 68:19 "For you have not received the spirit of bondage again to fear but you have received the spirit of adoption, whereby we cry Abba Father." I Peter 3:9

When we cry out to God, He says "do not be afraid for I am with you; do not be dismayed, for I am your God. I will strengthen you and help you; I will uphold you with My Righteous Right Hand. For I am the LORD, Your God, who takes hold of your right hand and says to you, DO NOT FEAR; I will help you." Isaiah 41:10,13 "The LORD is on my side; I will not fear: what can man do unto me? He is my helper." Psalm 118:6 "The LORD is my light and my salvation whom shall I fear? The LORD is the stronghold of my life whom shall I fear? The LORD is the stronghold of my life whom shall I be afraid?" Psalm 27:1

"God is our refuge and strength, an ever present help in trouble. Therefore we will not fear, though the earth may give away and the mountains fall into the heart of the sea." Psalm 46:1-2 There are many more promises in the whole chapters of Psalms 34, 121, 91

Therefore, "let us fix our eyes on Jesus, the author and perfector of our faith " Hebrews 12:2 KJV "Who will keep you in perfect peace, you whose mind is steadfast because you trust in God." Isaiah 26:3 "For the mind controlled by the Holy Spirit is life and peace." Romans 8:6b In these promises, we live our lives as witnesses of our Savior, Jesus Christ, "who is glorified in you, and you in Him, according to the grace of our God and the LORD Jesus." 2Thessalonians 1:12

"May the LORD of PEACE Himself give you peace at all times and in every way. The LORD be with you." II Thessalonians 3:16

My Thoughts

Communicating with God

P rayer is communicating and communing (talking) with God our Heavenly Father. To commune means to talk in an intimate way, which in prayer means to come to God, to listen for His Voice as we meditate during our daily quiet time.

"I will meditate on Your wondrous works." Psalm 145:5b "My soul yearns for You in the night; in the morning my spirit longs for You." Isaiah 26:9 "Be still before the LORD and wait patiently for Him." Psalm 37:7a "Come my children, listen to me: I will teach you." Psalm 34:14 "My sheep listen to My voice; I know them and they follow Me." John 10:27 "Teach me to do Your will for You are my God." Psalm 143:10 "I will instruct you and teach you in the way you should go. I will counsel you and watch over you." Psalm 32:8 "Whether you turn to the right or to the left, your ears will hear a voice behind you, saying, this is the way; walk in it." Isaiah 30:21

Meditate means to softly repeat over again and again what the LORD our Father has you focusing on in the word (the Bible): it could be just one word, or a phrase, or the whole verse. As you repeat the words of scripture they become a live in your body, soul and spirit.

My Thoughts

Look To The Lord

Look to the LORD and His strength; *seek His face always*
Psalm 105:4

November is the month of changes in Florida, when the days become cooler, the trees and plants begin preparing for the winter, and the tantalizing smells of food being prepared to celebrate. This is the month when many people think about their blessings of what they have, materially and spiritually.

We celebrate Thanksgiving with family and friends by preparing an elaborate dinner of turkey with all the trimmings. It is a day to offer thanksgiving for what our Heavenly Father has provided us with during the year. ***The LORD wants us to spend your time with Him this month in worship and praise.*** In your prayer closet spend most of the time praising and worshiping the LORD for He has given more than we could ever ask for. (I Timothy 6:17b)

Psalms were the praise hymnal of the early church and are still essential to our understanding of the presence of GOD's kingdom power in our lives today. Psalms are directly related to the practice of praising GOD. Singing/reading praises prepares a specific place (like a prayer closet) for GOD to be with us, His people (with you personally). (NKJV p.702) GOD our

Heavenly Father waits for this praise filled worship from us His believers. So with hands uplifted we exalt the LORD with our praise. (Psalm 63:4) Let us lift our hearts and hands to GOD in heaven. (Lamentations 3:41) Lift up your hands, and bless the LORD. (Psalm 134:2) While praising the LORD, we wait for Him and in His word we do hope. (Psalm 130:5) This we recall to our mind, therefore we have hope. Through the LORD's mercies we are not consumed, because His compassions fail not. They are new every morning. Great is Your faithfulness. (Lamentations 3:21-23) Hallelujah! Praise the LORD for loving us so much. We have a Heavenly Father who wants to be with us, His children.

Let us come before His presence with Thanksgiving; let us shout joyfully to Him with psalms. (Psalm 95:2) Let us give thanks and meditate on His words to us. Let the words of my mouth and the mediation of our hearts be acceptable in Your sight, O LORD, our strength and our Redeemer. (Psalm 19:14) Start a journal to write about all the wondrous provisions the LORD has provided for you each day. Write all the thoughts that come to mind during that time that you are spending with Him. In your journal tell the LORD how wonderful He is: for example this could be all the adjectives you can think of to describe your feelings for Him. Or in your journal write verses that you read which were meaningful from your reading during your quiet time. David who wrote most of the psalms in the book of Psalms sang and wrote all his feelings down so we would have examples on how to worship the LORD in praise. The psalms 135 and 136 are considered to be the great songs of praise while the psalms 120-134 are the Songs of Ascent that the people sang on their way to worship at the temple in Jerusalem. Read your thoughts from your journal or scriptures out loud to change the atmosphere to praise with joyous sounds to the LORD. Remember the enemy does not like to hear thankful, joyous believers singing and saying praises to the GOD of all creation. ***Who is like our GOD, among the gods? Who is like You, glorious in holiness, fearful in praises, doing wonders***? (Exodus 15:11)

For all things are for your sakes, that grace, having spread through the many, may cause ***thanksgiving to abound to the glory of GOD.*** (II Corinthians 4:15) ***Let's give thanks always for all things to GOD the Father in the name of our LORD Jesus Christ.*** (Ephesians 5:20)

My Thoughts

Blessing for A New Year

"God be merciful unto us, and bless us; And cause His face to shine upon us and among us; That Your way may be known upon Earth, Your saving power (Your deliverances and Your salvation) Let us praise You (turn away from their idols) and give Thanks to You, O God; Let all the people praise You" Psalm 67 Amp

January first starts a new year with everyone making New Year's resolutions on what they want to change during the year. Have you ever thought about making one for a closer walk with GOD. He is waiting and longing for you to make Him a priority in your life. Did you realize that "**because of His <u>great love for you</u>, God, who is rich in mercy, made you alive with Christ, making you a new creation.**" *"For you do not live by bread only, but by every <u>word</u> that proceedeth out of the mouth of the LORD."* When you make a new year's resolution to spend time with **GOD**, **"GOD says, 'I will put my spirit within you, and cause you to walk in my statues. You will be renewed in the spirit of your mind." "You were taught to put off your old self, which is being corrupted by its deceitful desires;** *to be made new in the attitude of your mind,* **and** *to put on the new self, created to be like GOD in true righteousness and holiness."*

Therefore, "Walk not as the Gentiles (unbelievers) walk in the vanity of their mind. So far as your former way of life is concerned; get rid of unwholesome talk, all bitterness, rage and anger, brawling and slander, along with every form of malice. Do not conform any longer to the pattern of this world, but be transformed by the renewing of your mind. In the morning, let the LORD hear your voice; in the morning lay your requests before Him and wait in expectation."

Make the commitment to daily "call on GOD, for He will answer you; give ear to you and hear your prayer. He will show the wonder of His great love, He will save by His Right hand those who take refuge in Him. He will instruct you and teach you in the way which you should go; He will guide you with His eye. Be careful how you live not as unwise but wise."

"May GOD be merciful unto you and bless you; and cause His face to shine upon you. May He grant you a spirit of wisdom and revelation (insight into mysteries and secrets) in the (deep and intimate) knowledge of Him. By having the eyes of your heart flooded with light, so that you can know and understand the hope to which He has called you and how rich is His glorious inheritance in the saints." Ephesians 2:4; II Corinthians 5:17; Deuteronomy 8:3; Ephesians 4:23; Exodus 36:27; Ephesians 4:23; Ephesians 4:17; Ephesians 4:17; Ephesians 4:4; Ephesians 4:29; Psalm 17:6; Psalm 32:8; Ephesians 5:15; Psalm 67:1 (Amplified); Ephesians 1:17-18 Amp

My Thoughts

Prayers, Intercessions, and Thanksgiving

For those who are "in Christ, not having your own righteousness which is of the law, but through the **faith of Christ** the Righteousness which is of God by faith." Philippians 3:9 It is our privilege to be able to call on God our Heavenly Father anytime. "I will call on You, O God, for You will answer me; give ear to me and hear my prayer." Psalm 17:6 "For great is Your love, reaching to the heavens; Your faithfulness reaches the sky. Be exalted, O God, above the heavens; let Your glory be over all the earth." Psalm 57:10-11 "**Listen to Him** who rides on the heaven of heavens, which were of old! Indeed, He sends out His voice, a mighty voice! Acknowledge that strength belongs to God, with His majesty over all of us and His strength in the skies. How awe inspiring is our God, from His Holy places, our God gives power and strength to His people. **Praise be to God!** Psalm 68:33-34 "Be joyful always; pray continually; give thanks in all circumstances, for this is God's will for you in Christ Jesus." I Thessalonians 4:16-18 Be joyful always, praying continually, and giving thanks in all circumstances is very hard to do. If you remember that you are to seek **first** the kingdom of God and His Righteousness and these things shall be added to you (Matthew 6:33), then it becomes easier to comply with scripture on how to pray. By going to God first, you are putting your trust in Him. You are saying God is greater than any situation or problem. "Be anxious for nothing, but in everything by prayer and supplication with thanksgiving let your requests be made known to God. Philippians 4:6

Now is the time for you to completely rely on God, your Heavenly Father, for any and all situations that are up setting you. God our Father has complete control of every situation. Now is the time "for prayers, intercession and thanksgiving be made for our leaders, and all those in authority, that you may live peaceful and quiet lives in all godliness and holiness. This is good and pleases God your Savior." I Timothy 2:1-3

Pray also that "the evil of the wicked will come to an end, and that God's Righteousness will be established, since only God is Righteous, testing the hearts and minds of all. My shield is God Most High who saves the upright in heart. God is a Righteous judge, who expresses His wrath everyday. Therefore I will give thanks to the LORD because of His Righteousness and will sing praise to the name of the LORD Most High." Psalm 7:10-11, 17

How wondrous to know that "God is my stronghold and a tower of strength **in times of** trouble. I, **who know God's name**, will put my trust in Him, for He will not abandoned me who seeks Him." Psalm 9:9-12

My Thoughts

Love One Another

Finally, all of you be of one mind, having compassion for one another, love as brothers, be tenderhearted, be courteous; not returning evil for evil or reviling for reviling, but on the contrary blessing, knowing that you were called to this, that you may inherit a blessing (I Peter 3:8-9)

L ove is advertised during the month of February in commercials, signs in the stores and especially in cards with hearts saying 'I love you' or 'will you be my valentine?' We as believers in Jesus, GOD the Father, and the Holy Spirit have the perfect love to share. We are the **LORD's examples of His love** "because the Love of GOD has been poured out in our hearts by the Holy Spirit who was given to us." (Romans 5:5) GOD's love is pure and holy without malice (desire to cause pain, injury, or distress to another) (I John 4:7-18) We show GOD's love through our actions and the words we speak. Words that we speak can be either a blessing or a curse. (Gen 12:3, Proverbs 4:20-22,) In our society today, people become easily offended by a look, a word that is spoken, behavior, or mannerisms. For example: many of us are offended at how people drive their cars either too slow, too fast, or cut in front of us, etc. The LORD asks us not to do the same by returning the same actions, but to bless the offending person as the LORD sees them. (Psalm 37:8, Ephesians 4:31-32)

"Blessing" is more than a mere formality, blessing has the power to turn lives around and make us into a blesser. "The Hebrew word for blessing is barak which simply means, to speak the intention of GOD for that person. In the New Testament eulogia (Greek) means "to speak the intention or favor of GOD on someone." (Strong's Concordance) Just as eulogies are tailor made, so are blessings

"Speaking a blessing over someone or something releases the LORD's power to work in their lives. This is a prophetic insight to see the way someone or something is supposed to be, not how they may appear to be at the moment. When we bless someone we are stating: "May the LORD grant you all of His intention for you or May GOD's full expectation for you be fulfilled in your life." (Jeremiah 29:11) When we choose to bless we are acknowledging that GOD's view of someone is greater than our own opinion." *The Power of Blessing* Kerry Kirkwood

In your prayer or quiet time ask the LORD to help you with how to bless those around you in everyday situations. A few suggestions are listed. Ask the LORD what scriptures to use for each situation. Every blessing in the scriptures was verbal one: GOD spoke, Paul spoke. The blessings were spoken out loud to change the atmosphere around the person or place.

I bless ___(name)_____ with the knowledge that the LORD never slumbers or sleep but will watch over you and keep you from stumbling. With this knowledge I bless _____ with the peace He gives you in knowing that He will never leave you or forsake you. (Psalm 121, Hebrews 13:5) **I bless**_____ with the renewing of a steadfast spirit within you to sing and praise to the LORD. Being grounded in the LORD you will continue to be steadfast in your faith that is the anchor of your soul. (Psalm 51:10, Hebrews 6:19)

I bless _____ with the banner of love over you. The banner of love will keep you safe in the arms of the LORD. (Song of Songs 2:4, I John 4:7-17)

I bless _____ with the joy of the LORD, for the joy of the LORD will be your strength. The presence of joy is eternal, may you be blessed with that joy. (Nehemiah 8:10)

My Thoughts

Every Good and Perfect Gift

"Every good and perfect gift is from above, coming down from the Father of the heavenly Lights, *Who does not change* like the shifting shadows." James 1:17

"Jesus is the same yesterday, today and forever." Hebrews 13:8 How awesome to have a God who loves us as His very own; who longs to talk with us, who **absolutely does not change His mind** or His promises to us. The scriptures from Genesis to Revelation have instructions on how to live, worship and communicate (pray, talk) with Him. His promises from Genesis to Revelation are "the same yesterday, today and forever" (Hebrews 13:8) for God our Heavenly stands by His Word.

"God the Father has given us according to Zechariah three places where prayer is to be made. The **first** place is in the church: corporate prayer, earnestly praying in the sanctuary; **second** is in every home: a prayer time with your family; and the third is your secret closet: a secret place that you have set aside to come into God's Holy Presence." Zechariah 12:10-13 David Wilkerson *Praying in the Closet*

Jesus said, "My house will be called a house of prayer" Matthew 21:13; Mark 11:17 Corporate prayer is the members of a church and other churches coming together in the sanctuary or any other location to pray with one accord for God's directions and blessings for the various programs what is on the heart of God the Father for His people. "All continued **with one accord** in prayer. We will give ourselves continually to prayer." Acts 1:14; 6:4 "Through one may be overpowered, two can defend themselves. A cord of three strands is not quickly broken." Ecclesiastes 4:12

Family prayer/study time is a time set aside for devotions and prayer. This time can be a short time of fellowship for family members to become a complete unit in agreement with the LORD. "If two of you on earth agree about anything you ask for, it will be done for you by my Father in heaven. For where two or three come together **in My Name**, there am I with them." Matthew 18:19-20

The secret closet is the time**, you** alone, set to come into God the Father's presence to be refreshed. "When you pray, go into your room, close the door and pray to your Father, who is unseen. Your Father, who sees what is done in secret, will reward you (answer your prayer). Matthew 6:18 In Acts chapter 10, we read about a man who with his family were devout and God-fearing, praying regularly to God. His prayers were answered when God sent Peter to minister to him and his family. "Even Jesus went out (by himself) into a mountain to pray, and continued all night in prayer to God." Luke 6:12 "During this time the Holy Spirit will teach you and will remind you of everything I (Jesus) have said. "Peace I leave with you, My peace I give unto you." John 14:26-27

"For God did not give us a spirit of timidity but a spirit of power, of love and of self-discipline." II Timothy 1:7

"May the eyes of your heart be enlightened and may the Spirit of wisdom and revelation give you knowledge to know Him better." Ephesians 1:16-17

My Thoughts

Do You Have Anxieties

Have you longed for peace in your life? Are anxieties causing stress in your life? **God our Heavenly Father has promised us peace.** Peace that will "hem you in, behind, and before," Psalm 135:5, surrounding you in the comfort of the Holy Spirit. This is "the peace of God which transcends all understanding, guarding your heart and your mind in Christ Jesus." Philippians 4:7

God our Heavenly Father has said, "I will keep you in perfect peace whose mind is stayed on me: because you trust in me." Isaiah 26:3 Jesus said, "in Me you may have peace. In this world you will have trouble. But take heart! I have overcome the world" John 16:33 "Therefore come **boldly** unto the throne of grace, that you may obtain mercy, and find grace to **help in time of need."** Hebrews 4:16 "Wait on the LORD: be of good courage, and He shall strengthen your heart: **wait**." Psalm 27:14 "Be anxious for nothing but in everything by prayer and supplication, with thanksgiving, let your requests be made known to God." Philippians 4:6 "Be strong, do not fear; your God will come, He will take care of you." Isaiah 35:4 "I will listen to what God the LORD will say; for He promises peace to me." Psalm 85:8 Praise His Holy name for the love and peace He is surrounding you with by saying, "I will be joyful always; praying continually; giving thanks in all circumstances, for this is God's will for me in Christ Jesus." I Thessalonians 5:16

"A heart at **peace** gives **life** to the **body"** Proverbs 14:30 "A faith and knowledge resting on the hope of eternal life, which **God, who does not lie**, promised before the beginning of time." Titus 1:2

My Thoughts

A Valentine from You to the LORD

God the Father is sending you a Valentine
"I have loved you with an everlasting LOVE:
therefore with loving kindness have I drawn you to me"
Jeremiah 31:1

"GOD is LOVE! This is how GOD showed His love among us: He sent His one and only Son into the world that we might live through Him. This is love; not that we loved GOD, but that He loved us and sent His Son as an atoning sacrifice for our sins. If anyone acknowledges that Jesus is the Son of GOD, GOD lives in him and he in GOD." I John 4:9-15

He is waiting for you to send Him a valentine that says, **draw me, I will run after you, I will be glad and rejoice in you, I will remember Your love more than wine."** Song of Solomon 1:4 **"As the deer panteth after the water brooks, so panteth my soul after You, O GOD. My soul thirsteth for You (God), for the living God: when shall I come and appear before You?"** Psalm 42:1-2 KJV **"Unto You, I lift up mine eyes. My lips shall utter praise unto You. O how I love Your law (word): it is my meditation all day. How sweet are Your words unto my taste! Yea, sweeter than honey to my mouth."** Ps 123:1; 119:97,103,17

<u>GOD says to you</u> "gather to Me, My faithful ones, those who made a covenant with Me by sacrifice, the ones who give true thanks, who offer a sacrifice of thank offerings to Me, and fulfill your vows (promises) to the MOST HIGH. And call upon Me in the day of trouble. I will deliver you, and you will honor Me. Whoso offereth praise glorifieth Me: and to you who ordereth your conversation (talking to others) aright prepares the way, will I show the plan of GOD. Psalm 50:5, 14, 23 KJV **Therefore, "be strong and don't let your hands be weak, for your work (prayer/study time) will be rewarded."** II Chronicles 15:7 **"I will draw you with cords of a man (human kindness), with bands of love."** Hosea 11:4 **Therefore I, "the Lord your GOD am with you, I am mighty to save, I will take great delight in you, I will quiet you with My LOVE, I will rejoice over you with singing."** Zephaniah 3:17

"**And the Spirit and the bride say, 'Come!' And let him that hears say, 'Come!' And let him who thirsts come. And who-ever desires, let him take the water of life freely."** Revelation 22:17 KJV

My Thoughts

This is the day
the LORD has made

Have you thought about being **devoted in prayer**, in communion with GOD our Heavenly Father as a constant part of your life? *"They all joined together constantly in prayer."* Acts 1:14 *"They devoted themselves to apostles' teaching and fellowship, the breaking of bread and to <u>prayers</u>."* Acts 2:42

Praying constantly should be a continual part of our spiritual lives as breathing is a part of our physical life. You can talk/pray all day telling the LORD how the day is going and to ask His thoughts concerning your daily activities. For instance: when going for your early morning newspaper, have you thought about lifting your eyes to the heavens and telling GOD how much you love Him; praising Him for loving you; asking for His blessings and directions on the coming day; asking GOD to help you put Him first in your thoughts and actions for the day. As you are preparing for the day, you can thank and praise the LORD for your house, food you are eating, or to ask His blessing on the day to help you continually to listen for His voice. **"This is the day the LORD has made; let us rejoice and be glad in it. O LORD, save us; O LORD, grant us success."**

Psalm 118:24-25 *"Build yourselves up in your most holy faith and pray in the Holy Spirit."* Jude 20

"And pray in the Spirit <u>on all occasions</u> with all kinds of prayers and requests." Ephesians 6:18 *"Watch and pray so that you will not fall into temptation."* Matthew 26:41 *"Let all those that seek thee rejoice and be glad in thee: and let such as love thy salvation say continually, let GOD be magnified."* Psalm 70:4 KJV

The more we devote ourselves to prayer/communicating with GOD, the closer we come to Him, so that in good and bad times, we know that *"HE (GOD) will keep in perfect peace him whose mind is steadfast, because he trusts in You."* Isaiah 26:3 *I(GOD) will strengthen you and help you; I will uphold you with My Righteous Right hand."* Isaiah 41:10b

"HE is a rewarder of them that diligently seek HIM." Hebrews 11:6 KJV *"Draw near to GOD and He will draw near to you."* James 4:5

My Thoughts

Freedom

The Freedom to gather, the freedom to worship, the freedom to pray

"proclaim liberty throughout the land to all its inhabitants." Leviticus 25:10

"I wait for you, O LORD, give ear to my words and consider my sighing. Listen to my cry for help, my King and my God, for to You I pray, And lay my requests before you and wait in expectation." Psalm 38:15, 5:1-3 "For surely the arm of the LORD is not too short to save, nor His ear too dull to hear." Isaiah 59:1 We stand on Your promises to hear our cries for mercy concerning our nation and the turmoil it is in, and will proclaim those promises aloud.

"The Founding Fathers proclaimed united public prayer and fasting days to honor God, thereby laying the foundation for the culmination of Isaiah 58:12, 'and they that shall build the old waste places: shall raise up the foundations of many generations; you shall be called, the repairer of the breach, the restorer of paths to dwell in.' History has demonstrated that the results of fasting promised in Isaiah 58 were achieved by the Pilgrims who set the foundations of this country on Biblical principles. Both spiritually and politically, they raised up the foundations of many generations." Derek Prince *Shaping History through Prayer and Fasting*

It is now up to us to unify with other believers to repair the breaches in our society. No matter what our political persuasions are, now is the time **for all** believers in Jesus Christ to come together in corporate prayer and fasting for our nation. (Psalm 133) By setting aside time for corporate fasting, prayers, and watches, we can prayerfully fight against the darkness, distress, and confusion that is overcoming our nation.

As we come before You, our Heavenly Father, let us offer thanksgiving and praise for what You are going to do in these coming months (Psalm 50:14). "Oh give thanks to the LORD, call upon His name, sing to Him, sing psalms to Him; telling of all His wondrous works! Glory in His Holy Name. Let the hearts of those rejoice who seek the LORD!" Psalm 105:1-3

We pray, O LORD, that You will illuminate (expose) by shining Your light upon the situation of our nation. (Ephesians 5:13) We ask You, O LORD, to bring out into the open what is hidden, that the words and decisions made in the dark (behind closed doors) will be made known to all in the daylight (to the public). And the words whispered in the ear in the inner rooms will be proclaimed from the roofs (media). (Luke 12:2-3) We pray the media will present an unbiased account of all news.

Let us pray that the Spirit of the LORD be upon us and our nation and for His banner/standard to be lifted up against the enemy's darkness that comes like a flood trying to cause fear and distrust in different people groups. (Isaiah 59:19-21

Let us pray that there will be unity between **all** believers with hearts fully committed to the LORD our God, and who will be willing to live by His decrees and obey His words. (I Kings 8:61)

My Thoughts

I Will Stand My Watch

"Be on guard! Be Alert!
"Be on guard! Be alert!
What I (Jesus) say to you, I say to everyone.
Watch!" Mark 13:33,37

I will stand upon my watch, and set me upon the tower, and will watch to see what He (God) will say unto me." Habakkuk 2:1 This is a time to seriously consider being a watchman/watchwoman in prayer for the direction of our nation. Now is the time to seriously spend time alone with Abba our Heavenly Father, praying for our national government, state and county governing bodies. Pray for a government in all branches to be based on Biblical principles of a people who will look to God our Heavenly Father for directions as the events seem to be spiraling out of control.

"The words watchmen, watchman, watch, watching, watchful, watcher and watches are mentioned 165 times and if you include see or observe or other words that have the same meaning as watch or watchman, you will find this subject mentioned 300 times in the Bible. We are all called to be watchmen/women, someone who watches God; who is attentive and listens to His voice; who obey His voice and leading of the Holy Spirit." Tom Hess *The Watchman*

"He who has an ear let him hear what the Spirit says to the churches" Revelation 2:29; 3:22 "Devote yourselves to prayer, being watchful and thankful." Colossians 4:2 "Be always on the watch, and pray" Luke 21:3, 6-7a The enemy doesn't want you to spend time being a watchman/woman for God. Prepare yourself for this battle by "putting on the full armor of God. For your struggles are not against flesh and blood, but against the spiritual forces of evil in heavenly realms. Stand your ground Stand firm." Ephesians 6:10-17 "Enter Abba Father's gates (prayer closet) with thanksgiving and His courts with praise; give thanks to Him and praise His name." Psalm 100:4 Praising and worshiping the LORD blocks the enemies' attacks.

In His presence "Cry out in the night, as the watches of the night begin; pour out your heart like water in the presence of the LORD." Lamentations 2:19 You are encouraged to keep asking the LORD as the person in the next verse asked: "watchman, what is left of the night? Watchman what is left of the night? The watchman replies, 'Morning is coming, but also the night. If you would ask, than ask; and come back yet again.'" Isaiah 21:11-12 You are being asked to be a watchman/woman for every day and to continue on in prayer for our country, for elected officials, and for all people groups. Pray for all churches to be a shining light on the hill as witnesses to the surrounding area. (Matthew 5:15) "Stay and keep watch" Matthew 26:38 "Trust in the LORD at all times" Psalm 62:8

"The LORD will fight for you (prepare the way); you need only to stay still (watch and pray)." Exodus 14:14

Thank you LORD that the church will be strengthened and encouraged by the Holy Spirit, causing it to grow in numbers, living in the fear (reverence for the LORD) of the LORD. In the name of Jesus Christ. Acts 9;31

My Thought

Hear My Voice

**"Hear my voice when I call, O LORD;
Be Merciful to me and answer me
My heart says, 'Seek His Face.'" Psalm 27:7**

And God answers me with "**be still, and know that I am God**." Psalm 89:15 "For My Lamp watches the spirit of a person. It searches out your inmost being." Proverbs 20:27 "You are the temple of the living God; I (God) will dwell with you and walk with you." II Corinthians 6:16 "I have made My Light shine in your heart to give you the Light of knowledge of the glory of Me, your God, in the face of Christ." II Corinthians 1:9 "I will be your refuge when you are oppressed and a stronghold in times of trouble." Psalm 9:9 "I have Loved you with an everlasting LOVE: therefore with loving kindness have I drawn you to Me." Jeremiah 31:1

I reply, how awesome to be in Your presence O LORD. "Create a clean heart within me, O God, and renew a steadfast spirit with in me." Psalm 59:10 Thank you for "restoring to me the joy of Your salvation and granting me a willing spirit to sustain me." Psalm 94:19 Thank you, Holy Father, that you will protect me by the power of Your name, the name You gave Jesus, so I may be one as You and Jesus are one. (John 17:9-12) "My heart leaps with joy and gives thanks to You in song" of praises for what You have done for me, Psalm 28:7b "I will extol You, my LORD at all times; Your praise will always be on my lips." Psalm 34:1

Thank You LORD that the "grace of the LORD Jesus Christ and the love of God the Father and the fellowship of the Holy Spirit is within me." II Corinthians 13:14

"**The God of Love and Peace be with you**" II Corinthians 13:11b

My Thoughts

Fret Not, Faint Not, Fear Not

In your prayer time of communicating with God, your Heavenly Father, do you reflect on your fears and worries, to let Him take control of them? Someone once said that there are three keys to inward peace: **fret not**: because God loves you; **faint not**: because God holds you; and **fear not**: because God keeps you.

Fret not because God loves you. "So know and rely on the love God has for you." I John 4:16 "Do not be anxious about anything but in everything by prayer and petition, with thanksgiving present your requests to God." Philippians 4:6 "Do not fret for it only leads to evil." Psalm 37:8 "Cast all your burdens on Him because He cares for you." Psalm 55:22 Therefore, "banish anxiety from your heart." Ecclesiastes 11:10

Faint not because God holds you; "even there Your hand will guide me, Your Right hand will hold me fast." Psalm 139:10 "In His love and mercy He redeemed you, He lifts you up and carries you." Isaiah 63:9b "Our LORD God will carry you as Father carries his son." Deuteronomy 1:31

Fear not because God keeps you. "The LORD watches over you the LORD is your shade at your right hand." Psalm 121:5 Isaiah said, "the LORD spoke to me with a strong hand upon me, warning me not to fear as the people feared and not to follow the people's way. The LORD Almighty is the one you are to regard as holy, He is the one you should fear (have reverence), He is the one you should dread, and He will be a sanctuary in times of trouble." Isaiah 8:11-14 "Do not fear what they fear, do not be frightened." I Peter 3:14b "So do not fear for I am with you, do not be dismayed, for I am your God, I will strengthen you and help you. I will uphold you with My Righteous Right hand." Isaiah 41:10 "And you can cry out and be saved; in God you can trust and will not be disappointed." Psalm 22:5 We have a God who does not lie whose promises are forever. (Numbers 23:19, Titus 1:2) "In Isaiah 55:11, the LORD says "so shall My word be that goes forth from My mouth; It shall not return to Me void (empty), but shall accomplish what I please, and it shall prosper in the thing for which I sent it." "The LORD is with me; I will not be afraid." Psalm 118:6 "There is no fear in love or God, God's perfect love drives out fear." I John 4:18a

Therefore, "you will have no fear of bad news; for your heart is steadfast trusting in the LORD. Your heart is secure, you will have no fear; in the end you will look in triumph on your foes." Psalm 112:7-8

"Whoever is wise let him heed these things and consider the great love of the LORD." Psalm 107:43

My Thoughts

Names, Names, Names, Names

Formal names, informal names, first names, nick names, endearing names, everyone goes by a different name during their lifetime that fits the occasion. God has many names that He goes by in the scriptures, each name fits the occasion and gives a description/attribute of His name. As you read the scriptures during your quiet time notice how God is revealed to different people or in different situations. Try using the various names you find for God in your prayers. God the Creator of Heaven and Earth wants to have an intimate relationship with you. "He wants you to remember His love is more than wine." Song of Songs (Solomon) The whole book of *Song of Songs* is a love story between the LORD and His Bride.

Sometimes we need to be reminded that God is the lover of our souls. He loved us so much that He sent His Son to be the "propitiation for our sins; and not for ours only, but also for the sins of the whole world. Jesus became our advocate with God the Father." I John 2:1-2 He is our creator "for He has created your inmost being. Praise Him for you are wonderfully made." Psalms 139:13-14

Do you realize He has written your name on the palm of His hand? "I will not forget you, "I have engraved (written) your name on the palms of My hands." Isaiah 49:16 Did you know that God considers you precious? "I have redeemed you; I have summoned you by name; you are mine. You are precious and honored in my sight." Isaiah 43:1,4 You can call Him precious, also. God is our friend. "He has promised to never leave you nor forsake you." Hebrews 13:5b "When Moses asked God what shall I say to the people; you shall say unto them, the God of your fathers hath sent me unto you. Tell them "**I AM** who **I AM, I AM** sent you." Exodus 3:14 "**I AM** with you; be not dismayed; for **I AM** your God; I will strengthen you; I will help you; I will uphold you with the Right hand of My Righteous." Isaiah 41:10

"Great is the LORD, He is exalted over all the nations. Let us praise Your great and awesome name. He is Holy." Psalm 99:3 NIV **"Let's tell of the power of His awesome works, proclaim His great deeds, and meditate on His wonderful works."** Psalm 145:6,5 "He is our Rock and Redeemer" Psalm 19:14 "He is the Alpha and the Omega." Revelations 22:13

"I have called you friends." John 15:15 Are you calling Him friend? As you spend time in prayer/meditation on the scriptures, are you trying to use some of His different names that you had read about. "Let Him (God) kiss you with the kisses of His mouth, for His love is more delightful than wine." Song of Songs 1:2 "The LORD your God is with you, He is mighty to save. He will quiet you with His love, He will rejoice over you with singing." Zephaniah 3:17 **How Awesome!!!!**

My Thoughts

"Stand firm in one spirit contending as one man

For the faith of the gospel without being
Frightened in any way by those who oppose you."
Philippians 1:27

Now more than any other time in recent history do we need to seek God's face for every faze of our lives. The more time we spend with our Heavenly Father in our prayer closet will enable us to distinguish His voice from other voices (my sheep know my voice and follow me. John 10:16) as you pray for direction. "For our struggle is not against flesh and blood, but against the rulers, against the authorities, against the powers of this dark world and against the spiritual forces of evil in the heavenly realms. Put on the full armor of God so that when the day evil comes you may be able to stand your ground. Stand firm with the belt of truth around your waist, the breastplate of righteousness in place, with your feet fitted with readiness that comes from the gospel of peace, hold the shield of faith which will extinguish all the flaming arrows of the evil one, put on the helmet of salvation and the sword of the Spirit which is the word of God." Ephesians 6:12-17 "Whoever listens to me will live in safety and be at ease, without fear." Proverbs 1:33

Let's start with a commitment of desiring and setting aside more time to be in God's presence. "Do not be wise in your own eyes, fear (reverence) the LORD and shun evil. Trust in the LORD with all your heart and lean not on your own understanding; in all your ways acknowledge Him and He will make your paths straight." Proverbs 3:7, 5-6 "I, God, will uphold you with My Righteous Right hand when you seek Me. Isaiah 41:10 "Ask God for wisdom who gives generously to all without finding fault. Seek the wisdom that comes from Heaven which is first of all pure; then peace loving, considerate, submissive, full of mercy and good fruit, impartial and sincere." James 1:4; 3:17 "For wisdom will enter your heart and knowledge will be pleasant to your soul. Discretion will protect you, and understanding will guard you." Proverbs 2:10-11 "The LORD is good, a refuge in times of trouble. He cares for those who trust in Him." Nahum 1:7

"Therefore fix your (eyes) thoughts on Jesus," (Hebrews 3:1) setting aside a time to come into His presence; to talk (pray) and to study the scriptures in order to hear His voice in the coming days.

Thank you, LORD, that _____ will find rest in you only. I bless you with hope that comes only from the Heavenly Father, for He alone is your rock and your salvation. He will be your fortress so you will not be shaken. Thank you, LORD, that _____ can trust You in all times good or bad, and that _____ can run to You for refuge. In Jesus' name, I bless you. Psalm 62:5-6, 8

My Thoughts

GOD is my defense
I shall not be moved.

He is the rock of my strength and my refuge.
Psalm 62:6-7

Hallelujah Hallelujah Hallelujah

We can come into the presence of the King of Kings with our worship, praise and requests. "...For GOD is light and in Him is no darkness." I John 1:5 Let us praise Him in our quiet time for "delivering us from the power of darkness and conveying us into the kingdom of the Son of His Love in whom we have redemption through His blood." Col 1:13-14 "With the LORD's lamp shinning on your head, that is when by His light you can walk through the darkness." Job 29:3 "The hope we have as an anchor of the soul, both sure and steadfast, and which enters the Presence behind the veil." Hebrews 6:19 "We now can with boldness enter though the veil into the Holy of Holies by the blood of Jesus. We can approach our Heavenly Father who is sitting on His throne with Jesus on His right hand side. We can draw near His throne with a true heart in full assurance of faith, having our hearts sprinkled by the blood from an evil conscience and our bodies washed with pure water." Hebrews 10:19-23

In your quiet time, "give attention to My (The LORD) words, incline your ear to My sayings. Do not let them depart from your eyes. Keep them in the midst of your heart; for they are life to those who find them and health to all their flesh." Proverbs 4:20-22 "Let the light of the gospel of the glory of Christ, who is the image of GOD, shine on you. For it is GOD who commanded light to shine out of darkness, who has shone in our hearts to give **the light of the knowledge** of the glory of GOD in the face of Jesus Christ." 2 Corinthians 4:4,6 Let the light of our precious Savior surround you during the time you spend in His presence, so that your demeanor and face will show you have been in the presence of the LORD of LORDs, creator of us all. "Trust in Him at all times, O people; pour out your hearts to Him for GOD is our refuge. Psalm 62:8

"Your Spirit and soul, I bless with the great joy that comes from experiencing the presence of GOD, sensing Him watching over your life. I bless you with sensing the presence of GOD in those things which the world calls problems and pain. I bless you in the name of Jehovah Shammah, GOD who is always there for you." Sylvia Gunter *Daily Spirit Blessings*

"Who is like our GOD, Majestic Holiness, Glory and Righteousness,

Who is like our GOD, Unending strength displayed, Forever He will reign,

Who is like our GOD, Who is like our GOD, **No One**,

Come let us remember our GOD will never change, Let us remember His kingdom will remain,

Let us remember the power of His Name, No one above Him, beside Him,

There's no one like our GOD" Song *Who is like our God* by Dustin Smith in the album *Coming Alive*

My Thoughts

The Month of New Beginnings

The New Year starts with the month of January. It is considered the month for new beginnings; but new beginning could be any date or time you want to make a new beginning. January is considered because it starts the New Year after celebrating Christmas, Jesus' birthday in December. January is the month many people think about starting anew. Did you think about setting aside a specific time every day for just being with the LORD? A time when you would read a chapter or two in the Bible and talk with the LORD about what you read, what you think and how it makes you feel? GOD the Father, Jesus the Son and Holy Spirit want to spend time with you. They want you to know them personally as friends who will be with you in all types of situations. **Prayer is a relationship** not a religious activity. The LORD is a live, you are alive. Prayer is the meeting of two people: one human and one GOD talking about the matters of the heart and His Word, how it relates to you in everyday situations.

"GOD looks down from Heaven on the children of man to see if there are any who understand, who seek after GOD." Psalm 53:3 "If then you have been raised with Christ, seek the things that are above where Christ is, seated at the Right Hand of GOD." Colossians 3:1 There are so many treasures in the scriptures the LORD wants to share with you. One of the treasures

He wants to share with you is the throne room, the Holiest place (Holy of Holies) where GOD the Father sits and Jesus on His Right hand (Psalm 110:1) We have this privilege through the blood of Jesus, by a new and living way which He consecrated for us to be able to enter the Holy of Holies. (Hebrews 10:19-23)

During this special time you set aside to be with the LORD, this is when you learn what is on His heart and you talk about what is on your heart. The LORD loves to hear you read His scriptures out loud to Him. Reading them out loud makes what GOD is saying in the passages more meaningful to your body, soul and spirit. "Psalm 42 is an excellent example how someone can pray reading a scripture. First the writer talks to the LORD aloud, then a few verses later he talks aloud to himself, but he knows his only hope is to seek GOD in prayer. He refocuses himself on the promises of GOD and confronts his fears. (Romans 10:17) Faith comes alive by hearing the truth(Word), so the psalmist seems to be preaching to himself, being renewed in hope as he reviews who GOD really is." (NKJ Commentary p.720) At the end of the Psalm 42 verse 11, the psalmist comes to the conclusion "Hope in GOD; for I shall yet praise Him, the help of my countenance and my GOD."

Jesus spent time in prayer before each day. (Hebrews 5:7) There are 175 verses on prayer found in the Gospels. Prayer was very important to Jesus. His disciples wanted to learn how to pray. Luke 11 is a whole chapter on different types of prayers starting with the LORD's prayer being the guide on how to pray/talk with the LORD. The LORD says, "Blessed is the man, blessed is the woman, who listens to Me each morning, alert and responsive as I start My day's work. When you find Me, you find life, real life, to say nothing of My good pleasure." (Proverbs 8:34 Message Bible)

You can start your prayer time with the following verses:

"O GOD, You are my GOD; early will I seek You; my soul thirsts for You; my flesh longs for You in a dry and thirsty land where there is no water. When I remember You on my bed, I meditate on You in the night watches." I will say, "Bless the LORD, O my soul and forget not all His benefits: Who forgives all my iniquities, Who heals all my diseases." (Psalm 63:1,6; 103:2)

Your words really matter to GOD

My Thoughts

"Peace I leave with you,

My peace I give unto you" John 14:17

A re you feeling overwhelmed with worries concerning problems at work, in your personal life or the feeling of helplessness in dealing with family problems? Are you "looking to Jesus the author and finisher of your faith?" Hebrews 12:3 Are you looking to Him in the immediate matter that is bothering you?

"If so, He will be a gracious benediction of peace in and through you. But if you try to worry it out, you obliterate Him (His peace and tranquility can't reach you). Your attitude concerning your problem will or not let the Holy Spirit work in your life. The attitude must be of complete reliance on God. Any problem that comes between God and yourself springs out of disobedience. Any problem that is alongside you while you obey God increases your delight because you know your Heavenly Father knows and He will answer." Oswald Chambers *Utmost for His Highest*

Sometimes the feeling while under the stress of the problem is as the psalmist says in Psalm 38:4,22 "For mine iniquities are gone over mine head: as an heavy burden they are too heavy for me. Make hast to help me, O LORD, my salvation."

When driving your car, you put your trust in the brakes that they will stop the car quickly. You don't have an unconditional promise that your brakes will never fail. You expect them to perform the task without question. How much more do you have when you put your trust in Jesus, God the Father, and the Holy Spirit. "Jesus Christ the same yesterday and today and forever, so you can boldly say the LORD is my helper. I will not fear." Hebrews 13:8,6 God is saying the **promise**s I gave to Abraham, Isaac, Moses, David and the disciples are just as **good for you** as they were for them.

"He wants you to cast yourself totally on His promises. It is a commitment to believe that God is bigger than all of your problems and enemies. God wants faith that endures the ultimate test. A faith that won't allow anything to shake you from trust and confidence in His faithfulness. Your obedience to God reflects this belief." David Wilkerson *Have I not Commanded You?*

"Be strong and of good courage; be not afraid, neither be dismayed; for the LORD your God is with you wherever you go." Joshua 1:9 Therefore, "the mind controlled by the Holy Spirit is life and peace." Romans 8:6 "Trust in the LORD. Delight yourself in the LORD. Commit your problems unto the LORD. Rest in the LORD. The LORD will uphold you with His Right Hand." Psalm 37:3,5,7,24 "I love the LORD because He listens to my prayers for help. He pays attention to me, so I will call to Him for help as long as I live." Psalm 116:1-2

My Thoughts

A Precious Gift

"I, your Heavenly Father, want you **to open your hands and your heart** to receive this day as a precious gift from Me. By the time you rise from your bed, I have already prepared the way before you. Bring Me the gift of thanksgiving, which opens your heart to rich communion with Me. I am GOD, from whom all blessings flow, thankfulness is the best way to draw near Me. Song 1:4" *Jesus Calling* p.184 *"This is the day the LORD has made; let us rejoice and be glad in it.* Ps 118.24

As we draw near to GOD, the Heavenly Father, Jesus, our Savior, and Holy Spirit will bind us to them, drawing us with cords of love. "Unity is a triple braided cord; us with Jesus makes the three stranded cord unbroken. Ecclesiastes 4:12 With Christ our source and center of our lives, negative forces cannot pull us apart." (NKJ Commentary p.850) Jesus longs for us to know the oneness with one another that He has with the Father. (John 17:21-23) The closer we come to the LORD, the more we change becoming more Christ like in our thoughts and behavior. "Make a joyful shout to the LORD, serve the LORD with gladness. Come before His presence with singing. Know that the LORD, He is GOD; It is He who has made us, and not we ourselves. Enter into His gates with thanksgiving and into His courts with praise." Psalm 100:1-4 "To the praise of the glory of His grace by which He made us accepted in the Beloved. In Him we have redemption through His blood, the forgiveness of sins, according to the riches of His grace which He made to abound toward us in all wisdom and prudence." Ephesians 1:6-8 "**Praise**: approbation, commendation, approval. Praise expresses not only for what GOD does for us, but also for who He is, recognizing His glory.(NKJ Word Wealth p. 1645)"

"Bless the LORD, O my soul and all that is within me, bless His Holy name. Bless the LORD, O my soul, and forget not all His benefits; Who forgives all my iniquities, Who heals all my diseases, Who redeems my life from destruction, Who crowns me with lovingkindness and tender mercies, Who satisfies my mouth with good things, So that my youth is renewed like the eagle's. So great is His mercy toward me who fear (reverence) Him; As far as the east is from the west, So far has He removed my transgressions (sins) from me. The mercy of the LORD is from everlasting to everlasting. Bless the LORD, O my soul." Psalm 103:1-5,11,12,17,22

Thank you, LORD, that I will not lose heart. Though outwardly I am wasting away, yet inwardly I am being renewed day by day. For my light and momentary troubles are achieving for me an eternal glory that far outweighs them (troubles) all. In the name of Jesus Christ. 2 Corinthians 4:16-17

A prayer just for you:

Thank you, LORD, that You are a sun and shield to us, giving us grace and glory. For You have said You will provide for those who walk uprightly. We praise Your Name for being an everlasting light, to light our ways as we travel through the darkness of this world. The light of Your presence will uncover everything hidden and kept secret. Therefore, we will not fear those who have kept hidden and covered their plots against us, but You, O LORD, will reveal their plots and bring to the light. We understand that the fear of man and his secrets brings a snare but our trusting in the LORD shall make us secure. You are our GOD who has given us not a spirit of fear but a spirit of power and of a sound mind. We will praise and sing songs of Your wondrous acts for what You have done for us. In the name of Jesus our Savior. Psalm 84:11; Isaiah 60:19; Mark 4:22; Matthew 10:26; Proverbs 29:25; 2 Timothy 1:7; Ephesians 5:19

My Thoughts

Spring Time

Spring time! A time of rejuvenation, a time when earth seems to refresh itself by the flowers and planets seemingly coming alive again after the deadness and dreariness of the winter. The birds are singing their jubilant songs of gladness to welcome life coming back to the greening of vegetation and the blossoms and flowers bursting forth with color and fragrances. It is a time of preparation for us during this season that we also call Lent.

Lent is a forty day period set aside for a time of reflection and renewal. A time to prepare ourselves, to try again to spend more time alone with our Heavenly Father, GOD; Jesus who sacrificed Himself; the comforter, Holy Spirit. The bridegroom, Jesus, calls to His bride, us the believers, to "rise up, my love, my fair one, and come away. For lo, the winter is past, the rain is over and gone, the flowers appear on the earth; the time of singing has come, and the voice of the turtledove (Holy Spirit) is heard in our land. The fig tree puts forth her green figs, and the vines with tender grapes give a good smell. Arise, my love, my fair one and come away." Song of Songs 1:10-13 The LORD wants to have an intimate relationship with us that can only be had by our spending time alone with Him, listening to what He has to say to us. HE has a plan for us. (Jeremiah 29:29)

Lenten season is a time of renewal for us: repenting of thoughts against someone: anger, fear, not spending time with the LORD to name a few. (Renewal: implies a restoration, a freshness: a literal change in our thoughts) After repentance, The LORD doesn't want us "to be conformed to this world, but to be transformed by the renewing of your mind, that you may prove what is good and acceptable and perfect will of GOD." Romans 12:2 He wants us to be led by the Holy Spirit, to cultivate the fruits of the Spirit: joy, love, peace, patience, kindness, goodness, faithfulness, gentleness, self control. (Galatians 5:22) We are to GOD the fragrance of Christ among those around us, believers and nonbelievers. (II Corinthians 2:15) The following verses will help prepare you for this Lent season and prayer time:

Thank you LORD that when I confess my sins, You are faithful and just to forgive me my sins and to cleanse me from all unrighteousness. In the name of Jesus. I John 1:9

Thank you LORD that after repentance (contrite heart) You will create in me a clean heart, and will renew a right spirit in me. May my meditation be sweet to You. In the name of Jesus. Psalm 51:10

Thank you LORD that Your mercy is so great toward me who fear(reverence) You. Blessed is the LORD who forgives all my iniquities. As far as the west is from the east You have removed my transgressions no longer remembering them. In the name of Jesus. Psalm 103:11-12,3

Thank you LORD that I can sing of Your wondrous works, letting my heart rejoice when I seek Your Face. I will give thanks to You, my LORD and will call upon Your Name. I will make known Your deeds among the people. In the name of Jesus. Psalm 105:1-5

Thank you LORD that those who wait on You shall renew their strength; they will soar on wings like eagles; they shall run and not be weary, they shall walk and not faint. They shall stand on Your promise to always be with them, for You have said, I am Your God" Isaiah 40:31, 41:10

Thank you LORD, blessed are the people who know the joyful sound! They walk, O LORD, in the light of Your countenance. In Your name they rejoice all day long, and in Your righteousness they are exalted. For You are the glory of their strength, and in Your favor our horn (strength) is exalted. Psalm 89:15-17

My Thoughts

Who Are You Trusting

T rust in me, trust in me, trust in me, trust in me, softly sang the python, Kaa, to Mowgli lulling him into thinking that Kaa was his friend. Mowgli was so mesmerized by Kaa's singing that he willingly let the coils of Kaa go around him until Bagheera, Mowgli's protector, rescued him just in time.

This scene from the Jungle Book illustrates what is happening around us. There are many voices crying out, trust in me, trust in me, I have the solution to the problems of our country and how to solve the world's problems, too. So many voices coming at us that some of us say 'what will be will be' and we just sit there letting whatever will happen happen. The deceiver wants us to be misled and mesmerized by the voices he has orchestrated to be so loud that we don't know which way to turn.

We do have the solution, **prayer**, being able to talk with God the Father anytime about our concerns for our country, state and county governments. "Blessed is the person who listens to me**, watching daily** at My gates, waiting at the posts of My doors." (Proverbs 8: 34) This is the time to cry "out to the LORD in their trouble, and He saved them out of their distress. He made the storm calm, and the sea waves were still." (Psalm 107:28-29; MEV) We are to keep crying out for our country and its people, to "seek the LORD your God, and you will find Him if you seek Him with all your heart (mind) and with all your soul. (especially now) when you are in distress (troubled) and all these things come upon you in the latter days, when you turn to the LORD your God and obey His voice. He will not forget the covenant of our founding fathers." (Deuteronomy 4:29-31)

"Our founding Fathers made a covenant with God, founding our country on the Biblical principles. A covenant with God is a binding covenant forever. Therefore, **pray** for the healing of our nation from the divisions, our strife, our wounds, and from the shedding of innocent blood" Dutch Sheets *Appeal to Heaven*

Praying for our country is not a one time commitment, it is a commitment to pray every day until God the Father heals our land and there is unity among all people. Pray for the people to listen to the LORD, who says, "turn to Me with all your heart, rending your hearts and not your garments. To return to the LORD your God for He is gracious and merciful, slow to anger, and of great kindness; And He relents from doing Harm." (Joel 2:1-12)

"Wait on the LORD; be of good courage and He shall strengthen your heart; wait, I say on the LORD!" Psalm 27:14 "Continue earnestly in prayer, being vigilant in it with thanksgiving." Colossians 4:2

My Thoughts

End Notes

E. M. Bounds, *Prayer Focus,* (Samaritans Purse Quarterly Prayer Magazine).

*Our Daily Bread Devotional, (*July 2001)

God Bless America: Prayers & Reflections For Our Country, (Zondervan 1999)

Oswald Chambers, *Prayer a Holy Occupation,* (edited by Harry Verploegh, Discovery House Publishers, 1992 Limited edition)

Oswald Chambers, *My Utmost For His Highest,* (Barbour Books, 1963)

Rolf Garborg, *The Family Blessing,* (White Stone Books, 2003)25-27

Derek Prince, *Mother in Israel, Lydia Prince,* (Derek Prince Ministries, 1971)

The Spirit Filled Life Bible, New King James Version, Commentary Kingdom Dynamics word study, 701-702

Kerry Kirkwood, *The Power of Blessing,* (Destiny Image Publishers, Inc. 2010) *21*, 31-33

David Wilkerson, *Praying in the Closet,* (World Challenge Publications)

Derek Prince, *Derek Prince on Experiencing God's Power,* The chapter on *Shaping History through Prayer and Fasting*, (Whitakerhouse, 1999)371

Tom Hess, *The Watchmen,* (Progressive Vision International/ Jerusalem House of Prayer for All Nations 2000) 4-5

Sylvia Gunter, *Daily Spirit Blessings,* (The Father's Business, Birmingham, AL 2005) Day 6

Dustin Smith, *Who is Like Our God,* Song from the Album *Coming Alive*

New Spirit Filled Life Bible, *New King James Version*, Commentary Kingdom Dynamics 720

Oswald Chambers, *Utmost for His Highest,* (Barbour Books, 1963)

David Wilkerson, *Have I Not Commanded You?* (Word Challenge Ministries)

Dutch Sheets, *Appeal to Heaven,* (Dutch Sheets Publications, 2015)

Sarah Young, *Jesus Calling,* (Thomas Nelson, 2004) 184

The Spirit Filled Bible, *New King James Version*, Word Worth, 1645

The Spirit Filled Life Bible, *New King James Version*, Commentary Kingdom Dynamics, 850

CPSIA information can be obtained
at www.ICGtesting.com
Printed in the USA
BVHW041936121221
623864BV00013B/840

9 781498 488662